What People Are Saying About Jack R. Taylor and *Cosmic Initiative*...

When I read *Cosmic Initiative*, it made me realize how blessed I am to call Jack Taylor my friend. Here is a book you won't be able to put down, because it focuses on things that matter when it comes to the Christian faith. It is written by a person who loves Jesus Christ, is unashamed of the Holy Spirit, and whose sole aim in life is to glorify God. Every sentence mirrors this commitment. Every sentence will draw you closer to God.

—*R. T. Kendall*
Author of sixty books
Former Senior Minister, Westminster Chapel, London

Twenty-five years ago, I was struggling to pastorally lead the church toward cultural relevance and gospel impact. A man who is deeply loved and admired humbly advised me that the only way to be consistently relevant was to seek and find the Kingdom. He was right! Today, I lead an international mission organization challenged by multicultural environments in more than seventy countries. Jack Taylor's advice those many years ago served to prepare me for this assignment. May *Cosmic Initiative* produce in you the same insatiable hunger that all "Kingdom adventurers" share for comprehending and agreeing with God's eternal rule and reign.

—*Bill Snell*
President, Missionary Ventures, International

In a world that is whirling in political crisis and turmoil, there is nothing more restorative, calming, and faith-building than picking up this book, *Cosmic Initiative*, and rediscovering that the Kingdom of God is the ultimate victor over Satan, fallen man, and all international chaos. Thank God for the Kingdom and for Jack Taylor's revelation of it!

—*Charles Carrin*
Charles Carrin Ministries, Boynton Beach, FL

Too often, the books we read are like a trickle from a clear, cool spring; we drink from them and are a little refreshed, a little less thirsty, but are left knowing that only more can satisfy. In contrast, reading *Cosmic Initiative* is like standing under the deluge of Niagara Falls! There is so much revelation to take in at once. One must revisit the pages pouring from the eternal, gushing river flowing from the Father's throne. Who could be trusted to pen the heart of eternity's Initiator? Who could sit before the expanse unfettered by time and space to describe the boundless Kingdom? And what could possibly describe God's intent? Jack Taylor is that man. *Cosmic Initiative* is that book. Are these words too great, too much, even overreaching? Only if Jack Taylor is less than I know him to be. Only if *Cosmic Initiative* is less than what heaven demanded.

—*Brian Higbee*
Author, *Living the Kingdom Life*
Senior Leader, CityChurch, Connellsville, PA

Jack Taylor's first book, *The Key to Triumphant Living*, was the very first book I was given that gave understanding and revelation that there was much more to the Christian life and relationship with Jesus than what I was currently experiencing. Since that day, Jack Taylor's books, teachings, and writings have been a guide to me in a remarkable, transformative journey that is beyond anything I could have imagined.

It is with great joy that I recommend Jack Taylor's book, *Cosmic Initiative*, as the crowning achievement of his life of revealing the heart of God to His creation. This deep yet clear revelation of the centrality of the Kingdom of

God to all that He is about in this world will assist you in getting the big picture of the Father's heart and purposes for us, which are much grander and more powerful than we could ever imagine. I will be including this book as required reading in our school here at Global Awakening, and I recommend it highly to you!

—*Mike Hutchings, DMin, ThD*
Director, Global School of Supernatural Ministry and
Director, Global Healing and Prophetic Certification Programs
The Apostolic Network of Global Awakening

COSMIC
INITIATIVE

JACK R. TAYLOR

COSMIC INITIATIVE

RESTORING THE KINGDOM, IGNITING THE AWAKENING

WHITAKER
HOUSE

COSMIC INITIATIVE:
Restoring the Kingdom, Igniting the Awakening

JackRTaylor.com
Dimensions Ministries, Melbourne, FL

ISBN: 978-1-62911-806-2
eBook ISBN: 978-1-62911-807-9
Printed in the United States of America
© 2017 by Jack R. Taylor

Whitaker House
1030 Hunt Valley Circle
New Kensington, PA 15068
www.whitakerhouse.com

Library of Congress Cataloging-in-Publication Data (Pending)

1 2 3 4 5 6 7 8 9 10 11 ɯ 24 23 22 21 20 19 18 17

This volume is dedicated to…

Friede:
my wife and "one heaven of a woman!"

My children and grandchildren:
Tim and his wife, Michelle; Blake and Brice
Tam and her husband, Bill Snell; Clay, Chris, and Tim
Kim and her husband, Mark Adams

My three great-grandsons:
Aiden, Austin, and Cashton

*And a growing host of hungry people with ravenous appetites for that
ultimate something worth dying for.*
Until we find that something worth dying for, we are not apt to
find anything worth living for. The truth this book addresses is
precisely the only reality worth dying for because it is the
summation of all reality:
THE COSMIC INITIATIVE

THE REASON I WRITE

When we preach, we carve in vapor;
When we write, we carve in stone.
What we preach will be forgotten;
What we write lives on and on.

These simple lines from an unknown author have escorted me
through hours of glorious and laborious writing.

CONTENTS

FOREWORD BY BILL JOHNSON

Cosmic Initiative has captured the heart and message of Jesus in a way that will capture your heart and transform your life. Here's why.

This past week, I had a conversation with someone who was lamenting her upbringing. There was no mention of ungodly parents or of abusive spiritual leaders in her church. From the sound of it, she was raised in a normal Christian environment where the message of salvation was preached week after week. Strangely, the very power and beauty of the message of salvation have caused many people to think that is all there is when, in fact, our salvation introduced us to a Savior who is also a King. And everything finds its purpose and fulfillment under His rule, which is called the Kingdom of God. Her sorrow was that only now, in the latter part of her life, had anyone told her about the Kingdom. You see, once the Kingdom is seen for what it is, it defines everything else.

The good news of the Kingdom of God was the message that Jesus preached, as did the apostle Paul and other New Testament writers. And most important for us, it was the message Jesus commissioned us to preach. By declaring the message of salvation in Jesus, we bring the opportunity for salvation to those who are listening. In God's economy, the declaration is what brings that reality into the room. So what happens when we preach the message of the Kingdom of God as a present reality? It ushers in the realm of His rule, on earth as it is in heaven. Everything dramatically changes in the environment of His reign.

Tragically, the message of the Kingdom of God has been so marginalized that many who teach it are thought to be out of balance at best and cultic at worst. Books have been written and programs have been broadcast to undermine this message. These efforts are aimed at bringing the believer back into a "balance" that Jesus neither taught nor practiced. All of this activity seems to be driven by fear, fueled by an unwillingness to recognize that more could be available to us than what we presently know. Take note: fear-driven posturing contains neither power, love, nor a sound mind. (See 2 Timothy 1:7.) On the other hand, the evidence of the Holy Spirit's presence and influence is liberty! The enemy of our souls does not want us to discover the fruit of this message.

In the same way that the Pharisees saw Jesus as a threat to their position of power and influence, many leaders today are threatened by a possible shift in theological position that might imply we've not been as successful in life and ministry as we could have been. The fight to protect the sanctity of our past has kept us from entering a more significant future. Additionally, a desire to be rescued from the darkness around us by the return of Christ has dulled our appetite to fulfill the assignment He gave us in the Great Commission. Make no mistake, Jesus' return to earth will be glorious beyond anything we could possibly imagine! But our faith should be applied to the power of the gospel of the Kingdom. It's time to believe the message Jesus gave us to preach, and to preach it boldly, for He is looking for us to bring Him the fruit of our labors—the transformation of entire cities and nations.

Jesus frequently taught using parables. He did so to illuminate one aspect or another of His Kingdom. From stories about mustard seeds to pearls to treasures in a field—all were used as illustrations to draw us into the journey of a lifetime, one that will continue throughout eternity. Interestingly, His parables also hid truth from those who were too preoccupied with their own kingdoms to care about the one that was supreme. By so doing, they evaded responsibility for the truth they were unwilling to follow. But for many others, Jesus' stories and teachings awakened something deep inside, making them willing to sacrifice everything to find the one great treasure of the Kingdom.

Jesus taught the Kingdom and illustrated the Kingdom. He performed miracles to reveal that His realm had come, having a measurable effect on the surrounding world, which had been marked by the works of the devil. And the things in our world that were inconsistent with His realm were automatically driven away. Every time this happened, it provided an opportunity for people to abandon what was inferior for what was superior—for what Jesus came to announce: *"the Kingdom of heaven is at hand"* (Matthew 4:17 NKJV)!

Cosmic Initiative carries this message. It expresses the heartbeat of God. Warning: reading this book with a humble heart will make it impossible for you to stay as you are. This book is an answer to prayer. We must have this profound message spoken by those with uncommon credibility throughout the body of Christ. And there are few that can match the favor given to the author of this book, Jack Taylor. His decades of faithful service to the various streams of the body of Christ that contribute to the river of God have earned him the right to speak with unusual authority and favor, for he who has loved well is well-loved. My prayer is that due to the regard given to him, multitudes of believers will once again embrace the commission that Jesus gave us: *"And as you go, preach, saying, 'The Kingdom of heaven is at hand'"* (Matthew 10:7 NKJV).

I can personally testify that Jack Taylor has been a great strength and encouragement to me in ways that no one could possibly know. He understands what Jesus revealed when He taught us to pray, *"Our Father...: For Yours is the Kingdom..."* (Matthew 6:9, 13 NKJV). It's a Father's Kingdom—it's family. Once we've left the subject of family, we've left the subject of the Kingdom of God. Jack Taylor lives to be an example and an encouragement in a fatherly way to countless numbers of people like me. I am eternally indebted to him for this gift. And now the grace that he carries is released through this book to all who read it. Page after page gives the reader insight, inspiration, and an insatiable hunger for the unlimited "more" found only in God's Kingdom. I don't know what more we could ask for from a book than personal transformation.

Cosmic Initiative will no doubt be an instant classic, marking this century with divine purpose like no other. It will ignite the hearts of a generation to sell everything to buy the field. It is with great pleasure that I can say to you, "Read this book, prayerfully." And let us become the transformational generation that Jesus is longing for.

—*Bill Johnson*
Senior Leader, Bethel Church, Redding, CA
Author, *When Heaven Invades Earth* and
The Power That Changes the World

FOREWORD BY LEIF HETLAND

Cosmic Initiative, written by my spiritual father and best friend, Jack Taylor, is a masterpiece of excellent scholarship destined to become a classic. We do not hear a lot about the Kingdom at parties—it is not the juicy topic of the day. We do not hear a lot about the Kingdom of God at the local restaurant—it is not the buzzword of commerce. We do not hear a lot about the Kingdom at election debates—it is not at the top of today's news. We don't even hear a lot about the Kingdom in our churches—it is not a hot topic of discussion.

Yet from the moment you begin to spend time with the author, whom I call "Papa Jack," it takes only a few moments before his passion for the Kingdom of God introduces you to the fullness of your citizenship in this heavenly realm. Papa Jack is Kingdom-possessed and is spreading a Kingdom virus that is highly contagious and will surely lead to a Kingdom epidemic.

In the year 2000, I was invited to attend a father and son meeting outside of Melbourne, Florida. It was during a wilderness season for me, a dark night of the soul, a winter season (or whichever way you describe it), and one of Papa Jack's sons, Dennis Jernigan, told me, "Leif, I have a song for you. It is a daddy's song."

As I listened to this song, for the next two hours I experienced what I call waves of liquid love. These waves continued to wash over me as I lay on the floor, totally undone by the Father's love for me. The voice of the Father said, "Leif, you are My beloved son. I love you, and I am well pleased with you." I call this experience my "Baptism of Love."

Within six months of this happening, I was spending time with Papa Jack, and I asked him to tell me about the Kingdom and what it would look like when heaven invaded earth. Papa Jack looked at me and said, "Son, I do not know. All I know is that the Kingdom will only be entrusted through family. The Kingdom is a family business, and our Father wants to extend His business into every nation, tongue, and tribe through sons and daughters."

For the next five years, I became a student of the Kingdom. In early 2005, I spent several days with Papa Jack and Mama Friede, listening to revelation on the Kingdom. I left their condo in Florida with a treasure chest full of Kingdom wealth. I found out sometime later that after I left, Papa Jack looked at Friede and said, "That boy is in for a lot of trouble. He thinks you can study the Kingdom, but what he doesn't know is that the Kingdom is studying him! He thought he came to get the Kingdom, but what he doesn't realize is that the Kingdom is about to get him!"

In May 2006, after another five months of hell, I surrendered to King Jesus and His unshakable Kingdom. Every single thing in my life became part of the King's personal property. For the past ten years, I have been on a daily journey with Papa Jack as a Kingdom citizen immersed in a Kingdom culture called family. Through family, we are learning to live from heaven toward earth.

"Your Kingdom come, Your will be done, on earth as it is in heaven" (Matthew 6:10 NIV) is our prayer. *"Seek first the Kingdom"* (Matthew 6:33) is our priority. *"Preaching the gospel of the Kingdom, and healing all kinds of sickness and all kinds of disease among the people"* (Matthew 4:23 NKJV) is our passion. *"This gospel of the Kingdom will be preached in the whole world as a testimony to all nations"* (Matthew 24:14 NIV) is our purpose.

Jesus never stopped talking about the Kingdom; neither has Papa Jack. This book is a blueprint that empowers you to live as a Kingdom citizen.

As ambassadors of the Kingdom, we have a profound guide in *Cosmic Initiative* to live a naturally supernatural lifestyle in the Kingdom—a vision for which Jesus lived and died that will transform individuals, families, churches, cities, nations, and cultures.

For anyone who desires the key to experiencing heaven on earth, this book is a must-read. Its pages are full of Kingdom treasure, and I encourage you to seek it out. But chew it slowly, for it is a meaty substance.

—Leif Hetland
Founder and president, Global Mission Awareness
Speaker and author, *Seeing Through Heaven's Eyes*

A WORD FROM MY SON, TIM P. TAYLOR

I have had the double privilege of knowing Jack Taylor as my father both physically and spiritually—something I do not take for granted. My dad amazes me with his ability to continue to learn even after most people his age have long retired. He has written over a dozen books, and this will be his tenth book penned solely by himself. Hopefully, this will not be his last work, but will prove to be his most important book yet. *Cosmic Initiative* stands to eclipse all the rest, including his first book, *The Key to Triumphant Living*, which has over one million copies in print. This work is his most ambitious undertaking to date as it seeks to explain the unexplainable, describe the indescribable, and measure the immeasurable.

If you are unfamiliar with the Kingdom of God, you haven't met Jack! For the past twenty years, the Kingdom has been his obsession in a most healthy and inspiring way. He was the leader of the band for many people in discovering the Holy Spirit, and the foundation for even more to embrace a lifestyle of worship. This book will place him at the head of the throng that has been revived to pursue the Kingdom first!

The Kingdom of God is the central theme of the universe, and it calls us to discover it, to declare it as present today, and to demonstrate it with power on earth as it is in heaven. In my honest and unbiased assessment, Jack Taylor is one of the best authors I have ever read, and until you have read his take on any subject of spiritual significance, you have not considered all there is to know.

We have missed the alignment that only the Kingdom of God brings. Jack Taylor has discovered and now declares the divine power of the Kingdom that brings order to the chaos of this earth. It is the Kingdom that, once discovered, is our privilege to declare and our obligation to demonstrate in power to transform lives, homes, churches, communities, nations, and the world.

God is present, and His Kingdom is advancing. Will you be a part of the end-time harvest that will make the kingdoms of this world the Kingdom of our God and King? I pray that as you read this work, you will find heaven invading earth, just as we pray, *"Thy Kingdom come, Thy will be done in earth, as it is in heaven"* (Matthew 6:10 KJV)! Read this book at your own risk; doing so may be hazardous to your status quo!

—*Tim P. Taylor*
Son, co-laborer, and publisher
Dimensions Ministries and Burkhart Books

PART 1

CULTIVATING A COSMIC
(KINGDOM) VIEW

1

OUR COSMIC CONNECTION

A bout twenty years ago, I discovered what I have come to view as the truth of all truths. By this, I mean the one certainty among the multitude of truths in the universe that encompasses all the others. It is the overarching truth that refreshes, refines, and enhances the other truths as it sheds light on genuine reality.

Putting the Pieces Together

This primary truth is like the image on the front of a jigsaw puzzle box that shows what the completed picture will look like. Before we begin to put together a jigsaw puzzle, we have only scattered piles of small, uncelebrated pieces that have some meaning but are incomplete in their separateness. As we work on the puzzle, our eyes frequently glance from the individual puzzle pieces (and the parts we have been able to piece together so far), to the completed picture on the box. Determining to make sense of apparently unrelated parts, and persevering in the task, we slowly begin to see the formation of something recognizable. Our growing ability to see how the parts fit together touches our soul with a sense of satisfaction and success. By the end, we have taken many separate pieces and rearranged them, putting them into their proper position, thereby creating an image that replicates the original. All the pieces, in context, now make sense.

Working a jigsaw puzzle requires first beholding the big picture; then, progress and completion come by finding the pieces that make up the whole and fitting them into place. Likewise, what I discovered some years ago about the truth among truths—the overarching framework of the universe—is that it gives us a clearer picture of spiritual reality so that all the pieces of our life and faith can "fit" together as they were meant to, and in ways we never would have envisioned.

What is this all-encompassing truth? It is none other than the reality and centrality of God's eternal Kingdom. When we develop a Kingdom mind-set, we comprehend God's ultimate purposes for humanity and how He is accelerating those plans today. Knowing what we are really aiming for helps us to assemble our individual ideas and knowledge about God into a coherent whole, uncovering hidden spiritual purpose, giving accumulated biblical knowledge new meaning, and unlocking liberating truths.

Connecting with the Kingdom

From childhood, I have suspected that there was some kind of connection between life on earth and the greater universe. I was a little towheaded farm boy who lived so far out in the country that we hunted *toward* town. Growing up in the open spaces where the sky stretched high over the horizon, it was impossible for me not to notice its remarkable displays of beauty. There were no human structures or bright city lights to block my view of the night sky and its myriads of stars. I was so enamored with the star-filled heavens that I often found myself imagining being up there among them or traveling through them to the distant reaches of the universe. I faintly remember feeling that there was something or Someone greater out there to which, or to whom, I was related.

It wasn't long after I began stargazing that my "looking" turned inward, and I found my connection with that Someone greater when I received Christ at age ten and became related to the One upon whom the government of the cosmos has been placed. (See Isaiah 9:6.) But it would take many years before I recognized my true place in His cosmos—His Kingdom.

As a new believer, I soon felt a call to preach, and I yielded to this call at the age of fourteen, the same year I preached my first sermon (I have now been preaching for more than sixty-eight years!). This was the first step into a life I could not have imagined in my wildest dreams. To this day, I remember something of the mixture of terror and thrill that filled my soul at the thought that "little old me" was saved, forgiven, and, of all things, called to preach the glorious gospel of Jesus Christ.

I had a voracious appetite for truth—all forms of truth, but none was as keen, appealing, and attractive to me as biblical truth. Still, I had no one to disciple or mentor me. I didn't even know how to spell the word *disciple*, much less what it referred to. I had a wonderful father, but he was not a spiritual man. And I knew nothing about spiritual fathers, so I didn't even look for one to fill this role in my life.

Not only did I preach my first sermon at fourteen, but I also began to study for the ministry at that young age. Subsequently, I graduated from high school at fifteen and from college at nineteen. I married at twenty and immediately began my theological training. And I have been studying the things of God and His church ever since.

During much of that time, the structure of my theology was similar to those individual puzzle pieces I described above. I learned about atonement, regeneration, propitiation, justification, sanctification, and glorification. I explored eschatology (the study of last things), Christology (the study of Jesus, the Christ), theology (the study of God), pneumatology (the study of the Holy Spirit), soteriology (the study of salvation), and bibliology (the study of the Bible)—ad infinitum!

In the middle of all this, I was wonderfully filled with the Spirit and began to slowly understand the ways of God more specifically and personally. I learned about the "deeper life," the "higher life," the "Spirit life," and the "exchanged life." I treasured these truths, enjoying the rich spiritual benefits I received from them.

Looking back, I can do nothing but praise the Lord for my theological training and for being filled with the Spirit, but I still grieve to this day over the fact that I had no one to father me in the faith or teach me what was most important. I am therefore grateful that, one day, my heavenly Father opened to me the revelation of His Kingdom. With this experience, something shifted in my mind and in the depths of my soul, so that I began to see things in a new way. The reality of God's Kingdom and all that it involved began to ignite in me. It was all I could think about.

However, I had no place to put this exploding revelation among the multiple topics of my studies or even my experiences in the Spirit. Then I saw it! It wasn't supposed to "fit" among all the other parts of my theology because all those parts were just that: "parts" of the whole realm of God's character, nature, and reign, and my relationship with Him. I started to see the Kingdom of God as the center of my faith and theology, but even more than that, I saw it as "everything" that mattered and inclusive of everything I had ever known and everything I would ever learn about God and His sovereign rule. Little in the total landscape of my beliefs changed, but everything in my life began to take on a new order as ideas, convictions, and questions escalated toward what I now understand as the wholeness of a Kingdom perspective. What became the focus of my thinking cast its blessed shadow from center to circumference and brought new meaning to each individual part of the picture.

> With the revelation of God's Kingdom,
> something shifted in my mind and
> in the depths of my soul.

For example, when I first heard the good news that "God loves you and has a wonderful plan for your life," I was impressed by this message but clueless as to its full meaning. It had only slightly occurred to me that when I was saved, the life of God in Jesus Christ came to live inside me, and that I was suddenly a "house" where God the Father, God the Son, and God the

Holy Spirit lived. I certainly hadn't heard that the gospel was connected to a Kingdom that is larger than the universe, and that salvation ushered me into a "cosmic" realm and eternal connection with the Creator that would not only enable me to have fellowship with Him, but also fulfill my purpose of advancing His Kingdom on earth. I didn't have an understanding of God's eternal, omnipotent, and omnipresent realm—a view that now gave me a new way of living as it aligned the various elements of my life according to His will.

My story, and the stories of many others (such as the woman Bill Johnson mentioned in his foreword to this book), show that it possible to love God and be a Christian for many years but miss the true center of one's faith. We may understand an essential part, such as our much-needed salvation in Christ, but miss the key to personal and cultural transformation. Or we may understand many aspects of the Christian life, such as discipleship and the necessity of being filled with the Spirit, but still overlook its underlying reality and foundation. We may hear and proclaim the gospel of redemption in Jesus but not necessarily comprehend and communicate the complete *gospel of the Kingdom* that Jesus announced and demonstrated on earth. (See, for example, Matthew 14:14.)

I do not claim to be a prophet or even the descendant of a prophet (I can't find a single one in my family tree), but I venture to prophesy this: the greatest truths we will learn in future years will prove to lie just beneath the surface of what we thought we knew next to everything about, all because we have been reintroduced to the Kingdom of God through the Holy Spirit!

I have never lost my childhood fascination with the universe; it has only grown throughout the years. As I revisit scenes in my memory of that little country tyke lying on his back, his body resting in the cool grass of a summer night—sensing that he could somehow fit himself into that awesome, starry scene up in the sky—I remember feeling that making that connection would be a dream come true. I now know that what I suspected about reality at that time was well founded. I am more convinced than ever that what I envisioned at a young age about my inherent relation to the universe was correct—yet it goes far beyond my boldest, highest youthful expectations, and its spiritual reality is deeper than I ever imagined.

What Is the Kingdom of God?

I have learned much in the last twenty years of Kingdom study and experience. But do you know what? I still feel like a rookie when it comes to the Kingdom! I've discovered that an expanded understanding of the Kingdom must involve a continual readiness on our part to change our minds about many things, as well as to accept Kingdom revelation that leads us above our previous conceptions. Could this be the reason John the Baptist said, "*Repent, for the Kingdom of heaven is at hand!*" (Matthew 3:2 NKJV)? Or why Jesus Himself said, and I paraphrase: "Change your mind, because a new day has dawned, the Kingdom of heaven is here!"? (See Matthew 4:16–17.)

Developing a Kingdom mind-set begins with learning the nature of the Kingdom. The word *kingdom* itself begs definition, especially in a democratic society where the term is seldom used and even less understood. Any kingdom on earth includes three things: a king or queen, kingdom citizens, and the principles that characterize the relationship between the two. Or, to put it succinctly: a sovereign ruler; those who are ruled; and "rules." The Kingdom of God has those same elements, but on the highest plane, and His Kingdom exemplifies His divine nature and character. There are many kingdoms, but the Kingdom of God is one of a kind, and it is the only one that deserves the title "*the* Kingdom." For this reason, all references to God's Kingdom in this book are capitalized.

An Eternal Kingdom with Two Expressions

God is eternal, without beginning and without end; therefore His Kingdom is eternal. A proper definition of the Kingdom must actually be twofold—the present Kingdom and the ultimate Kingdom; or, as one author put it, the "now" and the "not yet." To begin, here is the definition of the ultimate, eternal Kingdom:

God's rule (reign) over everything and everybody, everywhere, in eternity, past, present, and future.

As it says in the Psalms,

*The LORD has established His throne in heaven, and His Kingdom
rules over all.*   (Psalm 103:19)

As we will see in coming chapters, the Kingdom of God is inclusive
of all reality, seen and unseen, telescopic and microscopic. Thus, we may
say with accuracy that God's Kingdom is nothing if not cosmic; it covers
all that exists, everywhere—past, present, and future; visible and invisible.

Additionally, the Kingdom of God is cosmic because it originates beyond the confines of our world. In my dictionary, *cosmos* is defined as a
"complete and orderly system."[1] Cosmologists have defined the universe,
or cosmos, as "all that is." While I agree with their definition, I really don't
think they are saying "all" in reference to *everything*, which includes not
only the totality of physical realities like matter, heat, energy, gravity, and
biological life, but also the totality of unseen spiritual realities that cannot
be measured by the physical senses or empirical methods. Thus, "all that is"
is much more than what can be experientially observed or detected.

Next is the definition of the present Kingdom:

The emerging order of God through Christ in the affairs of humankind on earth.

Even though I have presented two definitions, it's essential to understand that there are not two separate kingdoms but one heavenly Kingdom
with differing expressions in eternity and time. In its ultimate expression,
the Kingdom of God is eternal; there has never been a time when it did not
exist, and there will never be a time when it ceases to exist. In its present
expression, the Kingdom is the manifestation on earth (often hidden from
human senses, but revealed to those who are spiritually attuned) of what
has always existed in eternity past: namely, the rule of God as Creator and
Sustainer of the universe—what the late Myles Munroe called "God's Big
Idea."

The Kingdom's manifestation on earth began in the heart of God, as
did the entire physical universe—life, light, matter, time, order, and everything else. Creation was the scene of the visible, tangible beginning of

---

1. Michael Agnes, ed., *Webster's New World Dictionary and Thesaurus* (New York: Simon
and Schuster, 1996).

everything that exists in our world. God launched His sovereign rule over everything He created to live on the newly fashioned earth. Most significantly, He established the visible realm in order to found a family of human beings who would reflect His own person, purpose, and power. This family would immediately inherit and eventually inhabit the created world and, under the rule of their Creator, establish His government throughout the realm.

Early in the biblical record, God made these intentions for humankind clear and concise:

> God said, "Let Us make man in Our image, according to Our likeness. They will rule the fish of the sea, the birds of the sky, the livestock, all the earth, and the creatures that crawl on the earth." So God created man in His own image; He created him in the image of God; He created them male and female.   (Genesis 1:26–27)

Based on the above, let me now present this expanded definition of the Kingdom:

> The Kingdom of God is the eternal rule of God over everything and everybody, everywhere, for all time and eternity. It is above time yet envelops time; it transcends time and endures time. A million billion ages ago, God's Kingdom existed; a million billion years from now, it will still exist. Being eternally permanent, it wins the right to be called "everything," because everything else is either encompassed by it—or will ultimately cease to be.

Do you completely understand the words you have just read? I confess I don't! But I believe them with all my heart. I stand by my conviction that the Kingdom of God is supreme reality—and the greatest theme in the universe. Ultimate reality does not depend upon, and is not defined by, visibility or tangibility but upon permanence. In my view, the revelation of the Kingdom has almost completely disappeared from the eyes and ears of today's church. However, it has been present the whole time, ruling in the lives of those who have been willing to spiritually see it and hear it. Some of God's people have seen and heard it all along, and many more are beginning to see, hear, and speak about what they are now seeing and hearing!

I call God's purpose and plans for His Kingdom on earth His *cosmic initiative*. When I first sought to define the Kingdom many years ago, this description struck a nerve deep in my spirit. Because the ultimate Kingdom exists from eternity to eternity, the Kingdom has been present, though largely invisible, in every age of human history on planet Earth and in the cosmos. Thus, the ultimate Kingdom guarantees the existence of the present Kingdom. This poses no conflict to either expression. In fact, both complement each other, guarantee each other, and reflect each other.

> *The Kingdom of God is supreme reality and*
> *the greatest theme in the universe.*

Again, the Kingdom of God on earth exists because the eternal Kingdom has always existed. We do not lose one in pursuing the other. To pursue both expressions is to pursue the whole Kingdom. To focus on one expression to the neglect of the other is to do disservice to both.

God's Kingdom in the Affairs of Humanity

Because God is all in all and Christ is all in all, the Kingdom is all in all. I am becoming increasingly aware of why we call the gospel of the Kingdom "good news"! It's bigger and better than we ever thought or can fathom. And whatever God is up to, we are in on it. We are related as next of kin to the One who created everything and has made us to share is His eternal plans. (See Ephesians 3:20.)

Human history's greatest truth, therefore, is the reality of the Kingdom of God on earth. We were designed by God, our Creator-King, to be children in His royal family, and to rule with Him in His Kingdom. This book is your invitation to an amazing journey of discovering the Kingdom of God and all it offers. To enter into the life of God's eternal realm, where its sights, sounds, and sensations will shatter the borders of your consciousness and probe the length, depth, and breadth of your imagination. This is not the pursuit of a single spiritual "experience," no matter how helpful and healing those can be. This is a commitment to a process of Kingdom transformation that will never cease but continue and expand throughout eternity.

A Vast Kingdom Landscape

In the physical realm, I am continually captured by the various masterpieces God paints in His sunrises—all similar, but none exactly the same. On my iPhone and computer, I have hundreds of photographs of sunrises that defy sameness and ignite my anticipation of seeing a new "original" every morning. Similarly, I am joyfully overwhelmed at the new landscape of the Kingdom I see that challenges my imagination every day. I know I am part of God's great cosmos, His Kingdom—and so are you and everyone else who has a relationship with our Creator-Father through His Son, Jesus Christ.

In the decades since I first discovered the all-encompassing truth of the Kingdom, I have been filled with sheer joy and increasing excitement and expectation. This is the reason I can say to you now, as Jesus did when He first proclaimed the message, "*The time is fulfilled, and the Kingdom of God is at hand*" (Mark 1:15 NKJV)! Even now, the landscape of the Kingdom is becoming increasingly clearer to me; the high privilege of relating to the Father-Creator is growing more captivating; and my part in God's order seems even more riveting. I hope that you will feel the same as you progress through this book. Welcome to what I pray will be some "highs" as you discover Kingdom insights. But much more than that, I pray that when you come down from those highs, you will walk and talk Kingdom for the remainder of your life!

A Kingdom Prayer

I conclude this first chapter with the following prayer, which has been posted on my bookshelf at eye level above my computer throughout the writing of *Cosmic Initiative*. Before you picked up this book to read it, you were prayed for many times that you would receive the revelation of the Kingdom. I believe my prayers have already been answered. God says, *"Even before they call, I will answer; while they are still speaking, I will hear"* (Isaiah 65:24).

Lord, bless the life of the one whose hands open the cover of this book and turn its pages with a powerful anointing to relentlessly pursue not only the King, but His Kingdom and its truths written here, and the vast, boundless and borderless realm of truth that will be unfolding into the ages of eternity! In Jesus' name, amen.

2

THE CENTRALITY OF
THE KINGDOM

Seek first the Kingdom of God and His righteousness, and all these things will be provided for you.   (Matthew 6:33)

Jesus never declared *"Seek first..."* about any pursuit or purpose except for the Kingdom of God. The Kingdom was the central message of His teaching and ministry on earth, and that of His disciples. In the New Testament, the term *"Kingdom of God"* appears nearly seventy-five times, and its synonym, the *"Kingdom of heaven,"* appears about thirty-five times.

The Kingdom of God is not only *at* the center of reality; it *is* the center of reality—both visible and invisible; *moreover*, it includes all of reality, from center to circumference. In view of this, there are many reasons for us to make the Kingdom of God the center of our lives and faith. In this chapter, we lay a foundation on which we can build this strategic position by looking at what I consider the three most noteworthy of those reasons:

+ Scriptural Testimony
+ Logical Testimony
+ Personal Testimony

Scriptural Testimony

The Kingdom of God is not only the grandest theme in the universe, it is the grand theme of Scripture, shedding light on every biblical truth and revealing the highest relevance and deepest meaning of those truths. It has been said that when one aspect of truth is so deeply held, so fiercely defended, and so universally applied as to treat it like all the truth, to the exclusion of other truth, it can become as dangerous as an untruth. Such an approach is the source of many a heresy. The Bible contains thousands of truths, all valid, but not all equal. As we study the Bible, we need wisdom and anointing to "rightly divide," or correctly handle, the Scriptures. (See 2 Timothy 2:15 KJV, NKJV, NIV.) We must be able to recognize the value of the individual parts that make up the whole, without fixing on them to the point that they obscure the whole, which is the Kingdom. The Kingdom of God encompasses all the truths—it does not compete with them. This fact cannot be overemphasized.

Throughout the Bible, the centrality of God and His Kingdom is either asserted or implied, from verses like *"In the beginning God created the heavens and the earth* [or universe]" (Genesis 1:1) and *"Love the LORD your God with all your heart, with all your soul, and with all your strength"* (Deuteronomy 6:5), to *"Seek first the Kingdom of God and His righteousness"* (Matthew 6:33) and *"The kingdom of the world has become the Kingdom of our Lord and of His Messiah, and He will reign forever and ever!"* (Revelation 11:15).

The very first passages of the Bible are bursting with expressions of God's authority and raw power, showing that His Kingdom is the warp and woof of creation. The Genesis record declares the supremacy of the Kingdom in its inaugural manifestation on earth. The God who existed in the beginning, from eternity, created the world. The very words that describe the process of creation ring with the sounds of purpose and possibility—the adventure of extending the Kingdom to earth had begun! The whole scenario speaks eloquently of a Ruler over a realm, those who are ruled, and the rules, or principles, that define the relationship between them.

The seminal nature of these opening passages of Scripture informs every issue of human history. I therefore make the following suggestion: When you have sufficient time and space to allow God to let you in on what He is up to with His Kingdom, open your Bible to the first chapter of Genesis. This is a Book about Him and His rule in relation to you and me—and everyone else who has lived, is living, or will live on earth. He had us in His mind when His Spirit hovered over creation and when He crowned His creation by forming humanity and making clear His reason for that act. As God's plan for human beings continues to unfold, it remains the greatest story ever told.

After you have considered all this, gently close your Bible and hold it in both hands, thanking God for it, because within it is the answer to every question worthy of an answer. It is the manual of the Kingdom of God, and it answers the vital question, "Why center on the Kingdom?"

Logical Testimony

If we affirm, based on Scripture, that God is God and there is no one above Him, then He is sovereign over all, and we may draw certain logical conclusions consistent with that premise. I call these rational conclusions "God's Bill of Rights." God's right to rule has multiple aspects, so each succeeding point in this section simply speaks of the breadth of His reign. Here, then are God's Bill of Rights:

The Right of Sovereignty. God, who was and is the summation of all reality, has freedom in His sovereign Self to do what He desires.

The Right of Rule over Creation. Since God is the Maker of the universe and all created beings, it is reasonable to deduce that He is greater than everything He has created, and that the greater (the Creator) rules over the lesser (the creation).

The Right of Purpose. As Creator and Ruler over heaven and earth, God alone is free to do with His creation as He wishes. Thus, even now, He is carrying out His eternal purposes for the totality of creation. Those who claim that God does not exist and who avow the folly of any thought of a divine presence are heralds of a parade of hopelessness. Their "gospel" is the following: human beings are nothing more than matter in motion. The soul? A product of fantasy. The afterlife? A myth. Human purpose? A massive illusion. Is such a mind-set not a good place to insert the centrality of the Kingdom of God and humanity's purpose in it?

The Right of Love: "God *is love*" (1 John 4:8, 16). Since God *is* love, loving others is something He inherently does. Love entitles God, as the One who loves, to rule with love, and it entitles us, the loved, to receive and respond to His love. His pure love, together with His total sovereignty, gives Him the right to rule in our lives.

The Right of Redemption: God has the right to rule over all whom He has personally redeemed in Christ: "...*the church of God, which He purchased with His own blood*" (Acts 20:28). The first verse of this much-loved old hymn captures this indispensable point:

> Blessed assurance, Jesus is mine!
> O, what a foretaste of glory divine!
> Heir of salvation, purchase of God,
> Born of His Spirit, washed in His blood.[2]

The Right of Providence. God has the right to be our main Provider, the One we are to look to first for all our needs. Jesus said, "*Seek first the Kingdom of God and His righteousness, and* **all these things will be provided for you**" (Matthew 6:33). One of the names for God in the Old Testament is *Jehovah-Jireh,* meaning "the God who provides." (See Genesis 22:14.) According to *Strong's* concordance, the word *Jehovah-Jireh* literally means "Jehovah will see (to it)." I think the ideas of *providing* and *seeing* converge well here. God provides on the basis of what He sees is needed—and He sees all. His provision involves His full vision and His total care.

To be sure, there are other logical conclusions we could make regarding the various facets of God's sovereignty, but the above should be sufficient to establish an understanding of His all-encompassing rule.

Personal Testimony

The third reason to make the Kingdom of God the center of our lives and faith is the personal testimony of those who have experienced the Kingdom and are convinced of its reality. Such testimonies are worthy to

2. Fanny J. Crosby, "Blessed Assurance, Jesus Is Mine," 1873, *Hymns for the Living Church* (Carol Stream, IL: Hope Publishing Company, 1974).

be shared with others; however, we should note that no matter how compelling they are, they fall short of sufficient evidence to prove to others the correctness of a position such as the centrality of the Kingdom. To assert, "I have found this to be true for myself, and I know it is also applicable to others since I am exceedingly satisfied with its results" may sound interesting to your hearers, but more evidence is needed for them to be fully satisfied. (One such evidence may be the hearers' own personal experiences.)

Though personal testimony may not be the strongest reason to support the centrality of the Kingdom, it is certainly not an insignificant one. In fact, when all three factors are considered, personal experience is not only necessary but inevitable for those touched by the Kingdom. Thus, personal testimony is a strong complement to scriptural testimony and logical testimony because it encourages us to listen to one another and learn what God may be teaching us. In addition, scriptural testimony and logical testimony can be used to evaluate such personal experiences.

> *Personal experience is both necessary*
> *and inevitable for those touched by the Kingdom.*

In chapter 1, I gave personal testimony about the revelation I received concerning the nature of God's Kingdom—that the Kingdom is the truth of all truths, the truth that encompasses all others. In this section, I want to share more about my personal experience in the ways in which God has progressively taught me about His Kingdom.

I wrote my first book, *The Key to Triumphant Living*, to chronicle the personal and corporate revival in the church I pastored in San Antonio, Texas, with its attendant results in the lives of individuals and churches. I briefly retell the story here, forty-five years later, for the purpose of identifying transforming truths that yield light on the Kingdom. The genesis of the awakening was my life-altering realization that Jesus, in the person of the Holy Spirit, was *alive* in me. This came at a time when I was deeply dissatisfied with my ministry. Yet with this heavenly revelation, my whole being exploded into a new level of awareness of spiritual things. Today, many years down the line, this seems quite elementary, but it was an episode that has affected my entire life and ministry.

The transformation can be traced to the day when I was reading the Scriptures and a very basic, common truth caught my eye: *"God wanted to make known among the Gentiles the glorious wealth of this mystery, which is* **Christ in you***, the hope of glory"* (Colossians 1:27).

How can I describe what happened next? Previously, if someone had asked me if I believed that passage, my answer would have been a quick affirmative. But this time, it was different. I rather suddenly discovered that the heart of my Christian experience was Jesus Christ as Lord, living in me in the person of the Holy Spirit.

Furthermore, until this awakening in our church, I was a certified "pneumaphobic" (I was afraid of the Holy Spirit's present work in the world). Radical Pentecostalism was the only movement with which I was acquainted that really had much to say about the third person of the Trinity, but their "antics" were too much for this Baptist kid. I had asked God to fill me with the Spirit, but I wanted the stripped-down version, just the standard equipment, so I could feel safe in a Baptist church.

Then we invited a retired Southern Baptist Missionary to speak to our church. Miss Bertha Smith had been a missionary to China until all the missionaries were expelled by the Japanese. (Most of these missionaries finished their mission careers in what is now Taiwan, then called Formosa.) Bertha Smith's ministry had been in the north of China in the Shantung Province. A mighty revival had broken out there, and all of our American missionaries had been filled with the Spirit. When "Miss Bertha," as she was affectionately called, came to speak to us near the end of 1969, she immediately asked three questions:

+ "Have you been born again?"
+ "Have you been filled with the Holy Spirit?"
+ "Are you being filled right now?"

By then, my desperation level for God had begun to rise above my fear level, and I wanted all He had for me—whatever the cost. Miss Bertha pressed for an answer to all three questions. The answers to the first two were easy at first, but when I scrambled for proofs of the Holy Spirit having filled me, I came up short. Sensing that the divine moment had come, Miss Bertha observed, "Pastor, I believe your folks are ready to 'pray through.'" This was a term I had only heard used by the Pentecostals. I knew what it meant, and about twenty of my congregation, most of them staff members and their spouses, along with my wife and me, retreated to the choir room to do business with God. We immediately began to pray, and the Spirit of God started to move. My associate pastor, who was our director of education, suddenly blurted out, "God, I want to be filled with the Holy Spirit, and I want to feel it when I comes!" Well, God obliged him, and he began to weep convulsively, a protocol I had never witnessed in him before.

My music director was next. He cried out to God—and God met him. My desperation now soared into the stratosphere. My praying went along these lines: "God, I am open to Your Spirit, and I have asked You to fill me, but I miss two things: joy and power."

As clearly as I had ever heard Him before, the Father spoke to my spirit, *Son, it's My Holy Spirit; you're still afraid of Him, which means you don't trust Him.* It hit me like a ton of bricks: *I had been fearful and distrustful of the only God who was on the planet, the Holy Spirit!* Before I could pull the card of orthodoxy and question the theology of that statement, I began to weep, and then to laugh helplessly.

Little did those present realize that we had all experienced something that would shape the remainder of our lives. Within four months, God came in a mighty revival that saw at least three thousand people swept into the Kingdom of God and believers move to a new level of their faith. Subsequently, a culture of spiritual awakening occurred that none of us had ever witnessed before. After a few years, I was led to an itinerate ministry to share what the church and I had experienced.

In coming years, I wrote other books that marked spiritual discoveries that proved vital to my following Jesus with both joy and power, including such topics as faith, prayer, spiritual warfare, the Holy Spirit and His gifts, deliverance ministry, the family, finances, prayer, our identity in Christ, and the integrity and infallibility of the Scriptures.

And then came a hiatus—no more books; it was "laboratory" time. While ministry continued and God's blessings attended, another component forced its (nearly) unwelcome presence into my life: heartache, suffering, pain, disappointment, and loss—including heart surgery with complications that seemingly brought death very near, and the sickness and death of my wife, Barbara, a wonderful woman who died in my arms after more than forty-seven years together.

My period of grief ended happily in a joyous marriage to Jerry. However, a diagnosis of cancer for Jerry had invaded our relationship during our engagement. Though the dread disease proved powerless to alter or weaken our love for one another, it was to make our time together too brief indeed. We married despite the presence of the unwelcome prognosis, and God gave us twenty-one beautiful and powerful months of marriage. Then she was taken from me, leaving me in greater grief than before. Yet I discovered grief to be not only an entitlement but an empowering experience. Those days of lingering loneliness drove me more deeply into God, leaving me with no part of my life untouched. Then Friede came into my life to provide the end to the parenthesis of pain and loss and the beginning of a period of unparalleled joy and delight in life and ministry.

> *God got my attention by establishing the glorious Kingdom in center position in my heart.*

I want to include one other life-shaping event only because of my lingering memories of pain and panic, misery and mystery, connected with it. I was in a tragic wreck in an all-terrain vehicle when I was on a mountaintop in North Carolina, in which I sustained extensive injuries: broken back, punctured lung, fractured ribs, and massive bruises, not to mention emotional distress. The frighteningly slow process of recovery took half a year.

I recount all these events and experiences as background to my saying this: through these episodes, I have discovered more and more of the treasures of the Kingdom of God. Such discoveries are difficult to describe or define, but I happily report today that God has used every adverse situation to construct a setting on which to mount a beautiful diamond that today defines my life in Him.

In everything I went through, God got my attention by unmistakably establishing the glorious Kingdom in center position in my heart and causing it to unfold in my personal life and ministry. As I wrote previously, I may not have much more *knowledge* than when this season of Kingdom discovery began, but the things I know, I know with *deeper certainty* and *greater expectation*, and I know them in the framework of the unfolding revelation of the Kingdom of God. I now know that all that happened was preparation for my discovery of the centrality and significance of God's eternal rule and of its implications in every aspect of our life on earth—and on into eternity. I can affirm that a restored understanding of the Kingdom has implications for all arenas of life and will lead to these results, and more:

+ A renewed sense of purpose for individual believers

+ A revitalized role for the church in the world

+ The healing of society's ills

+ The active proclamation of the gospel message with signs following

+ A hopeful view of the future of humanity

Scriptural testimony, logical testimony, and personal testimony— three vital reasons to make the centrality of the Kingdom the foundation of our lives and faith.

In this book, I have chronicled my deepest feelings and greatest expectations for our future in the Lord and in His Kingdom, for the purpose of causing you to love the King and His Kingdom more than ever and to seek the Kingdom as a present lifestyle. I ask you to think about your own journey in the Lord up to this point and reflect on how God may have been preparing you to understand the nature and potential of His Kingdom in your own life.

3

INSTRUCTIONS FOR YOUR KINGDOM JOURNEY

Having emphasized the centrality of God's Kingdom and invited you on a journey to seek the Kingdom, to understand it, and to live in its reality, I would like to give you some helpful instructions for the journey. Behind every good trip is a plan to reach the destination, as well as to stop at places of significance along the way, such as local attractions, natural wonders, and the homes of old friends we've too long neglected. A good map is helpful—notwithstanding the availability of GPS or an onboard computer. Travelers can't have too much information when they embark on a significant journey, and this is the most momentous journey of your life. Thus, the more information you have, the happier a traveler you will be.

I want this book to be a transformational tour of the Kingdom in which we are captured by the bigness of God, His love, His mercy, and His wisdom. I want our experience to be "out of this world" because we have an out-of-this-world God with out-of-this-world plans for us all. I encourage you to plunge your whole heart, soul, strength, and will into the journey. As we follow this path, we will never be the same; we will be changed, and we will continue to be changed forever and a thousand "evers" after that. The transformation within us will be so powerful that it will install the

King on the throne of our lives. Then, as in the New Testament, perhaps even our shadows falling over the sick, the lonely, the hopeless, and the violent will heal broken bodies, soothe volatile emotions, hush panicked hearts, and capture rebellious spirits for the Kingdom. (See Acts 5:14–15.) So keep focusing on the destination, heeding the signs that provide both information and caution, knowing that Someone is praying for you every word and every step of the way. (See Romans 8:26–28; Hebrews 7:24–25.)

Please read this chapter slowly and deliberately with an open mind and a receptive heart. Fasten in your mind the following three signposts for your Kingdom journey and return to these pages when you need encouragement and perspective along the way.

Three Signposts for Your Kingdom Journey

Signpost One: The Kingdom Is an Eternal Mystery

As we progress through our observations of the Kingdom, certain matters will be worthy of more than a passing thought, so they will be repeated. This first signpost is one of those observations to which we will return. God's Kingdom is a realm to be consciously entered; and, as the Kingdom is manifested through us, we will inevitably experience ongoing revelation and spiritual transformation. However, the Kingdom will always remain somewhat of a mystery to us—even after the end of time. This is because the magnitude of the Kingdom cannot be charted. No human instruments have the capacity to measure its length, breadth, depth, or height. It is simply inestimable and inconceivable! To attempt to process it with your best thinking will prove to be an exercise in futility.

The absence of a thorough comprehension of the Kingdom, however, does not mean the absence of your appropriation of it. It has been the Father's good pleasure to give us His Kingdom. (See Luke 12:32.) We just need to say, "Thank you!" in faith—and accept it. As we receive the Kingdom by faith, our faith will also prove to be the crucial element for the sustainability and growth of the Kingdom in us.

Furthermore, the Kingdom cannot be routinely addressed, assessed, or accessed by the unaided human mind because it is spiritual, eternal, and invisible, as well as the foundation of ultimate reality. Human logic and intelligence quotients notwithstanding, the mind of man, absent the enlightenment of God's Spirit in a redeemed spirit, has no clue regarding the mysteries of this realm. Consequently, we may engage in biblical studies that are accurate and produce a body of learning, but this knowledge, by itself, will be bereft of power. Historically, it has often happened that as certain unheeded or forgotten truths were being recovered, in the excitement of the season they were learned with the mind but never received as revelation. As a result, the truths took on a faddish character, and interest in the subject waned and died all too soon.

> *The reality of God's Kingdom will not be* taught
> *as much as it will be* caught.

We must remember that although comprehending the reality of the Kingdom of God involves the transfer of information, it will not be *taught* as much as it will be *caught*. Information, under anointed preaching, anointed study, and anointed listening will soon become *illumination*, which will lead to *transformation*.

The Kingdom yields the riches of its unfathomable mysteries to us only as the Spirit of God invades, penetrates, and transcends our human knowledge, bringing spiritual understanding that can be received and acted upon. The renewed mind, enlivened by and attentive to the Holy Spirit, can soar into the stratosphere of revelation as the breath of God begins to blow once more on the Word He first breathed millennia ago.

Additionally, revelation is essential to the effectiveness of ultimate spiritual truth as far as its ability to change individuals and the surrounding culture. An intellectual grasp of biblical knowledge alone cannot enable us to participate with God to redeem lost humanity from the spiritual, social, and political devastation now being globally encountered. The church must rediscover the centrality of the Kingdom of God if it is to gain this needed revelation.

This is why I give the following caution:

Do not seek to comprehend the mystery of the Kingdom as if human understanding must be achieved before you can receive and live out the Kingdom's transformational revelation.

One word anchors this vital truth: *infinite*. Being infinite, the Kingdom of God can never cease to be a mystery. However, the Kingdom is not hidden *from* us but *for* us for continual discovery! Thus, the quality of mystery will remain a part of our spiritual inheritance as we share in the unfolding of God's unsearchable riches throughout eternity.

In the process of writing this book, I have reviewed many resources on the Kingdom that I have collected through the years—including those in the documents sections of three different computers, a dozen and half flash drives, various PowerPoint presentations, powerful books on the Kingdom, and a stack of papers about a foot high—as I have searched for additional insights into the good news of the Kingdom. However, knowing that the Kingdom is an eternal mystery that must be revealed, I have also continually sought to listen for God's voice and allow Him to speak directly to my spirit. My keenest time for receiving revelation of the Kingdom is during in the night when I am suddenly awakened with two or three revelations from God so profound and pointed that I am almost shocked. Night can be the best time for me to obtain revelation because my mind has not sufficiently awakened to reason or argue with it. As God has breathed on my middle-of-the-night visitations with the Kingdom, I have often been so excited that I didn't even desire to go back to sleep!

Jesus' Kingdom is not of this world (see John 18:36); it is beyond this world. The naked eye cannot see the Kingdom's limitless reaches, and the naked ear cannot hear its ineffable glories. Allow the Holy Spirit to move upon you to reveal in your inner man the ultimate mystery of time and eternity. Celebrate this mystery, especially when your mind is boggled at the immensity of it all. We must seek the Kingdom regardless of its invisible qualities and even its puzzling features. I therefore encourage you to ask God for revelatory help as you read *Cosmic Initiative*. Take out your Bible and read for yourself the references I have included. Get accustomed to being periodically confused or even overwhelmed. Stop for a "wait-a-minute" break—you know, the kind in which you say to yourself (or to the author of this book), "Hold on a minute; I've never heard anything like that before, and I'm not sure I believe it. Let me think about it for a while!" It's all right to stop and think. I have surely had all the feelings, questions, and "aha!" moments you have had and will have.

When you come to a chapter or a section in this book that mystifies you—which may be expected—remember that it has probably mystified the author as well! Prayerfully read on, because later you will likely be moved to return to the scene of the mystery with new revelation and understanding. Take a deep breath and read on, praying as you proceed, "Jesus, help me to learn to live with mystery!"

Let me emphasize one further point: you may start out studying the Kingdom (King), but soon become aware that the Kingdom (King) is studying you! After a preliminary encounter with the reality of the Kingdom, one of my spiritual sons said, "Papa, I got it!" I replied, "No, it got you!" The fact is, if all that happened was that you "got it," you could lose it. But if the Kingdom (King) gets you, it (He) will never let go. You will start on an adventure of entering into a new lifestyle that mirrors that of our King.

So please heed this caution that I have been attempting to convey: stop trying to understand everything and begin with a decisive act of your will to receive the Kingdom from the Father. Think about the Kingdom until you develop a sense of awe for its King, and then simply praise the Lord for His reign, His might, and His majesty, and for your privilege of living in His eternal presence. Then you will be free to pursue the Kingdom of God undistracted by its magnitude and might.

Signpost Two: The Kingdom Is Our Calling

A Kingdom Tale

To convey the second signpost of the Kingdom journey, I want to tell you a story about a legendary moment in ancient history (into which I've incorporated some creative license). This story illustrates a deeply spiritual principle: we are called to seek and find the highest Kingdom in the universe. I call the following "A Kingdom Tale."

A man named Philonicus was a master horse trader. His steeds were mighty, and their prices reflected their great value. One of Philonicus's clients was a king in Macedonia named Philip, who bought a magnificent horse as a gift for his young son, Alexander.

This horse, called Bucephalus, was both beautiful and powerful. He was midnight black, with a white star in the middle of his forehead, and he had a brand on his left haunch with the likeness of a white ox. His head was huge and his body was massive, possessing the aura of pure might. His potent strength was evidenced when anybody tried to mount him. The king employed the best trainers to work with him and tame him, but they failed again and again. Finally, though he had paid a large sum of money for his prize steed, Philip declared the horse unmanageable and useless because no one could ride him. The horse was turned out to pasture, although from time to time, some trainers still tried to ride him—unsuccessfully.

One day, after yet another failed attempt to ride Bucephalus, Philip's son Alexander, who was about thirteen years of age, stepped forward and stated his intention to ride the mighty horse. Philip refused to allow him to. For days, Alexander pleaded and argued to be given a chance, and Philip finally relented and handed over Bucephalus's reins to his son.

Now, Alexander knew he was no ordinary lad. In fact, he had been told that he was a son of the gods, and he played the part to the hilt. His attempt at riding would surely be a spectacle worthy of everyone's attention and attendance, and a crowd gathered to watch. Unlike many others, Alexander was able to carefully mount the powerful horse. He fixed himself in the saddle, snapped the reins against both sides of the horse's neck, and gently kicked him in the ribs. Then Bucephalus began to snort and buck and leap, twisting in mid-air. The horse was determined to unload this rider as he had all the others. But the boy held on. The battle had begun!

Alexander was a precocious kid—confident, stubborn, and alert. In watching others attempt to ride Bucephalus, he had noticed that the horse would begin by making a slight movement with surprising speed, and then something invariably happened: he would go completely wild when he saw the shadow of himself and his rider on the ground around him. Knowing this, Alexander jerked the reins to the right, turning the horse until he was facing squarely into the sun. There were no shadows to frighten Bucephalus further, so the advantage slowly turned to his rider. Sensing success, his adrenalin flowing, Alexander snapped the reins again, kicked the horse in both flanks, and shouted in delight.

After a little more bucking, Bucephalus took off running and kept going until he was completely exhausted, with Alexander remaining steady in the saddle. Alexander then rode Bucephalus back toward the crowd of cheering admirers. The horse was panting furiously, and as Alexander dismounted, he gently slapped Bucephalus on his massive, sweating neck and smiled. Bucephalus seemed to understand, responding with his massive head, giving his conqueror a gentle, friendly nudge on the shoulder, as if to say, "Okay, I'm yours!" He had not only been conquered, he had been won over.

The king had been waiting for his son to dismount. Clearing his throat, and catching a tear tracing down each side of his face, Philip said, "My son, look for a kingdom worthy of yourself. Macedonia will never be large enough to hold you!"

From that time on, Alexander and Bucephalus were as one; each was an extension of the other. They were so close that they seemed to have a complete understanding of one other, almost as if they could read each other's minds. Alexander became renowned in the eyes of the whole kingdom, as well as in the eyes of the world. We know him as Alexander the Great.

After years of leading Macedonia's armies to manifold and powerful victories—mounted on his magnificent steed Bucephalus—and conquering the known world, he allegedly wept because he could find no other countries to conquer. Alexander had taken his father's words seriously and sought a kingdom large enough to match himself, his dreams, and his daring, and he found it. (Would to God the Alexander of history had found the eternal Kingdom, instead.)

The Kingdom Is Within You

I will never get over that moving story, and I hope the same will be true for you. I have spent some time and a bit of imagination to tell this legend about Alexander and his horse because I want you to remember and reflect on it as you hear our Creator-King say to you, clearly and often, "Don't settle for less than your destiny. Discover a Kingdom to match your own inner man—the Christ-in-you man! No human system will be large enough to stop you, because *'the Kingdom of God is within you'*!" (See Luke 17:21 NKJV, KJV.)

Repeat that mandate to yourself often so that it rings in your soul. You were made for the Kingdom of God—refuse to settle for any other. Don't allow any other kingdom or pursuit to win your loyalty, fill your passion, or distract your search for the greatest things in life. No other kingdom will answer life's pressing problems or solve the mystery of the reason for your existence on earth. No other kingdom is eternally relevant. When you seek first anything besides God's Kingdom, you are trafficking in nothingness, flirting with idolatry, and consorting with futility. Following any other kingdom, no matter how great and powerful it seems, will lead you to disappointment and dejection. And that other kingdom will merely pass away.

> *The Kingdom is not just a treasure, it is the treasure. When we have found it, we have found it all.*

Conversely, when you seek God's eternal Kingdom, you seek all that matters. The Kingdom has always been—and will always be—everything. The Kingdom is eternal, transcendent, and preeminent. There is nothing before and nothing after God and His Kingdom; both have no beginning and no end. There is nothing above, nothing beside, nothing beneath, and nothing other than the Kingdom. The Kingdom is not just *a* treasure, it is *the* treasure. Thus, when we have found this treasure, we have found it all.

Jesus taught us the key to life: *"Seek first the Kingdom of God and His righteousness, and all these things will be provided for you"* (Matthew 6:33). When we find the true Kingdom, we discover to our delight that everything else that is really necessary, helpful, and satisfying will be provided for us by our King. Furthermore, the Kingdom is inexorably connected with Jesus, who is our All in All, and in whom we are complete. (See, for example, Colossians 3:11.) The Kingdom is the ultimate, absolute reality because it has its existence and identity in Him. We must realize that what is true of the King is also true of His Kingdom. The two are inseparable. To think of One is to think of the other; to seek One is to seek the other. When we seek Jesus, we seek His Kingdom, which is the Kingdom of the Father. When we find the Kingdom, we find Jesus and His omnipresent reign.

Make it your goal, therefore, to seek and to find the one Kingdom that matches your essential, inner identity. You are a joint heir with Jesus, destined for the throne, the ruling center of the universe (see, for example, Ephesians 2:6), and you will reign forever with Him (see Revelation 1:6; Revelation 5:10)!

Signpost Three: The Kingdom Is the Whole

The word *axiom* refers to something that is universally accepted and widely applied as an evident truth. To highlight our third signpost, I would like to apply a well-known philosophical and scientific axiom to the Kingdom of God: "The whole is greater than the sum of its parts." As I emphasized earlier, the Kingdom of God is not just one truth among many truths. It is *the* truth of truths—the truth that encompasses the collective body of truth. If it is anything, it is everything. If it matters at all, it is all that matters. If it is not all that matters, nothing matters. (Have you noticed that I am trying to convey to you that the Kingdom is *everything*?)

Earlier, I used the illustration of a jigsaw puzzle to describe how, when we recognize the Kingdom as the whole, it enables us to better understand

and apply its various parts. Using the universe as another example may help to further clarity this idea. Imagine we took an excursion beyond earth and into space. We would see stars, planets, galaxies, nebulae—all moving at mind-bending speeds. We would see a billion galaxies, each with a trillion stars or more, and each a separate part of the universe. Our own celestial neighborhood, the great Milky Way, while huge in its own right, is but a tiny portion of this great whole. The universe illustrates our axiom well because, as theologian E. Stanley Jones noted, it is a *universe*, not a *multi*-verse. The parts are not unrelated but are all elements that belong to the greater cosmos. Additionally, we could even say that it is a "uni-" or single "verse"—or message—which says, *"God is!"*

As Creator, God spoke into being the entire ordered universe. And remember this: God's Kingdom is greater than and *includes* our vast universe. We have noted that the Kingdom encompasses everything visible and invisible in the created world, the telescopic as well as the microscopic. God's eternal reign is inherent in our very wide and widening universe, across millions of light years of space and time. One wonderful result of recognizing the whole of the universe is that of beholding the magnitude and magnificence of the God who created it.

In this imaginary journey into the universe, we have attempted to grasp the size of what God has created to function within His Kingdom that is material and tangible. But we also need to recognize something even more remarkable: God's Kingdom is a vast dominion comprising many individual parts belonging to the *spiritual* realm, as well as the physical world, each of them also contributing to the whole of the Kingdom.

Aligning Our Lives with the Kingdom

The main point for us to remember is that when we *see* the whole of the Kingdom, and then *align* ourselves according to it, then all the various parts of our lives will find their proper place, and we will be able to function as we were meant to operate in God's Kingdom.

Learning to see the whole of the Kingdom, as well as its various parts, will stretch our imaginations and understanding of reality to the maximum. Let us keep in mind what God says in Isaiah 55:8–9:

"For My thoughts are not your thoughts, and your ways are not My ways." This is the LORD's declaration. "For as heaven is higher than earth, so My ways are higher than your ways, and My thoughts than your thoughts."

God knows everything about everything; thus, His perspective and His ways are always right.

You and I do not know everything about anything; thus, our perspective and our ways are often wrong.

When our thoughts and ways do not line up with God's thoughts and ways, we need to change our minds to align with His. The more quickly we believe God's truth, turn around, and walk in His ways, the sooner we will enter into right thinking and right doing, which will, by the help of the Great Un-messer, "un-mess our messes." God rules over all, and everyone who bows to His rule comes into order with His purposes and plans. This is how we begin to "fit" into our proper place in His Kingdom.

You may ask, "How can I best respond to God's rule and move into His Kingdom order?" The answer to that vital question is in the passage immediately following Isaiah 55:8–9, which we looked at above. Here is my paraphrase of the next several verses:

"Just as rain and snow come down and water the earth and cause the seeds in the ground to germinate and sprout and ultimately bear fruit, so will My word be that is sent to do My will and finish its good work in you. Then you will have great joy: all nature will sing, and you will live a peaceful life that is ordered according to My will." (See Isaiah 55:10–12.) When we allow God's Word to flow into and through our lives, His thoughts and ways will become our thoughts and ways. The Kingdom lifestyle will become our lifestyle.

Additionally, this passage from the New Testament explains that the Holy Spirit will instruct us in God's purposes and desires:

The spiritual person, however, can evaluate everything, yet he himself cannot be evaluated by anyone. For "who has known the Lord's mind, that he may instruct Him?" **But we have the mind of Christ.**

(1 Corinthians 2:15–16)

We each have an essential role in God's grand, eternal plan—His *cosmic initiative*. God has deemed us fit to rule in His Kingdom, both in this life and throughout eternity. Think if it: we are in training for reigning! One day, all the disparate parts—people, nations, races, planets, galaxies, nebulae, even black holes and everything else—will fit together into an ordered whole, and we will reign with God forever. We just need to recognize and enter into His grand plan. The apostle Paul said,

> We are [praying] *that you may be filled with the knowledge of His will in all wisdom and spiritual understanding, so that you may walk worthy of the Lord, fully pleasing to Him, bearing fruit in every good work and growing in the knowledge of God. May you be strengthened with all power, according to His glorious might, for all endurance and patience, with joy giving thanks to the Father, who has enabled you to share in the saints' inheritance in the light. He has rescued us from the domain of darkness and transferred us into the Kingdom of the Son He loves.* (Colossians 1:9–13)

"Filled with the knowledge of His will in all wisdom and spiritual understanding." Let's expand on this idea. There is much talk today about the importance of having a proper worldview. While I agree with this, I am convinced that there is something even more important than a worldview—a cosmic view. I call this a "cosmic" view because it reflects the vastness of God's Kingdom and its realities. Generally speaking, a worldview has to do with planet Earth, but a cosmic view is a necessary extension to any worldview, because, as we know, the Kingdom of God contains the entirety of all reality, seen and unseen, in time and eternity.

Kingdom Repentance

Aligning our lives with the nature and purposes of the Kingdom requires a shift in thinking on our part, and this is an essential aspect of our repentance before God. I am not referring only to our initial repentance before Him. When we first come to God through Christ, our repentance has to do with recognizing our sin, sorrowing over it, and separating ourselves from it as we acknowledge that Jesus Christ paid the penalty for our sin, and as we receive Him as Lord and Savior of our lives. Included in receiving

Christ is a decision to choose God's way of thinking, adopting His will instead of ours.

Yet in its fullest sense, repentance—with the necessary component of humility—is a continuous decision to change our minds about anything on which we do not see eye to eye with God. Repentance, in this context, is not a onetime act but a lifetime commitment. When we live in repentance and humility, we are admitting to God our King, "I am helpless to know, experience, and implement the meaning of my existence and purpose in life, and I must have Your help. I am willing to change my mind [repent] of wrong thinking so I may receive the mind-set of Your Kingdom. Only Kingdom thinking and Kingdom living can overcome the effects of the fall of humanity, which has produced a worldwide culture of selfishness, greed, violence, and futility." It has never been more important for believers to adopt perspectives that are "out of this world." Only by adopting a cosmic view of everything can we be truly relevant in the world.

> *More important than a worldview is a cosmic view,*
> *because it reflects the vastness of God's Kingdom.*

Each of the three signposts we have explored in this chapter is vital for our Kingdom journey. Here they are in summary: (1) The Kingdom is an eternal mystery; don't try to understand it all before entering into its lifestyle. Just accept it, and you will receive—and continue to receive—revelation of the Kingdom. (2) The Kingdom is your calling; seek the only Kingdom that matches your essential identity as a co-heir with Christ. (3) The Kingdom's axiom is "the whole is greater than the sum of its parts." When we *see* the whole of God's Kingdom and *align* ourselves with it, all the parts of our life and faith can find their proper place, and we can function as we were meant to operate in the Kingdom.

As at the beginning of this chapter, I counsel you to return to these signposts and review them as you progress in your Kingdom journey. I believe you will find light to guide your way!

PART 2

RESTORING THE KINGDOM

4

THE GREAT COSMIC ROBBERY

Several years ago, I was visiting in the hospital with a longtime friend, Dr. Roy Fish, retired professor of evangelism at a prominent seminary from which, incidentally, we had both graduated at about the same time more than a half century earlier. I had just given Roy a copy of my favorite book on the Kingdom, *The Unshakable Kingdom and the Unchanging Person*, by E. Stanley Jones. During our visit, we drifted into a discussion about the Kingdom—always my topic of choice. When we paused for a moment in our conversation, the silence was broken by a very serious question from my friend: "Jack, why didn't we hear more about the Kingdom of God in our theological education?" I told him it was my conviction that there had been an intentional, methodical deception and theft of the Kingdom gospel, which had affected even our seminary. He agreed. This chapter is about that disastrous theft and how its effects reach to the present day.

The Gift of Kingdom Rule on Earth

In chapter one, we saw that the Creator established the physical universe and launched His Kingdom on earth for the purpose of founding a family of human beings who would reflect His person, purpose, and power. Under the glorious reign of their Creator, this family would administer

His government throughout the realm of earth. (See Genesis 1:26–27.) The delegated rule of humanity began in the garden of Eden, in which God placed the first man, Adam, and (soon afterward) his wife, Eve.

> *The LORD God planted a garden in Eden, in the east, and there He placed the man He had formed. The LORD God caused to grow out of the ground every tree pleasing in appearance and good for food, including the tree of life in the middle of the garden, as well as the tree of the knowledge of good and evil.... The LORD God took the man and placed him in the garden of Eden to work it and watch over it.*
>
> (Genesis 2:8–9, 15)

Adam and Eve were to be the keepers of the garden, cooperating with their Creator-King and being trained in their delegated rule by tending the plants, gathering the fruit, and nurturing the animals. What a great setup! Yet in His protective supervision, God warned Adam that while all the other trees in the garden bore fruit that was good for food and free for the taking (including the Tree of Life), there was one tree that was off-limits to humanity:

> *And the LORD God commanded the man, "You are free to eat from any tree of the garden, but you must not eat from the tree of the knowledge of good and evil, for on the day you eat from it, you will certainly die."*
>
> (Genesis 2:16–17)

Human beings were created to bear God's image and likeness, and to rule the earth under His authority. Adam and Eve were given the opportunity to trust and obey their Creator-King's instruction and warning—or to seek their own rule. Their tragic choice continues to cast its accursed shadow over the earth and heavens. Although we were designed and commanded to reign over God's entire creation, it must be understood that this reign has always been predicated on His reign over us. His sovereignty in our lives is what gives us reigning privileges and responsibilities.

In light of this, let us first look at the very, very bad news that resulted from Adam and Eve's choice, news that seems to grow even worse as time passes. Then we will come to the very, very good news, which will continue throughout eternity. It is necessary to examine the bad news in order for the good news to be fully relevant, reassuring, and redemptive for us.

I believe the great cosmic robbery occurred in two stages, and in two different forms. Stage one was the theft of humanity's God-given role in the administration of the Kingdom on earth; stage two was the distortion of the church's understanding of the Kingdom gospel after the Kingdom had been restored to humanity by Jesus. This misperception has been devastatingly effective in undermining the message and power of the Kingdom to this day.

Stage One of the Cosmic Robbery and Its Effects

Stage one of the great cosmic robbery occurred in the garden that God had given the first man and woman to live in, enjoy, and tend. Adam and Eve were unaware that the garden was about to become a battleground in an ongoing struggle over God's eternal Kingdom, which was being opposed by a lesser, but potent, kingdom ruled by Satan, or the devil. Satan had once been in God's service as a powerful angel named Lucifer, but he had rebelled, convincing a third of God's angels to join him. (See, for example, Ezekiel 28:11–17; Revelation 12:3–4.) The rebels were immediately expelled from heaven, but Satan still continued to wage war against God in whatever way he could. He now chose to further his cause by attempting to destroy God's Kingdom expansion plans for earth and humanity.

Going to Eve in the form of a serpent, Satan deceived her in regard to God's trustworthiness and intentions. She believed him, accepting his suggestion to eat from the prohibited *"tree of the knowledge of good and evil"* (Genesis 2:17), with Adam's complicity.

> [The serpent] *said to the woman, "Did God really say, 'You can't eat from any tree in the garden'?" The woman said to the serpent, "We may eat the fruit from the trees in the garden. But about the fruit of the tree in the middle of the garden, God said, 'You must not eat it or touch it, or you will die.'" "No! You will not die," the serpent said to the woman. "In fact, God knows that when you eat it your eyes will be opened and you will be like God, knowing good and evil." Then the woman saw*

that the tree was good for food and delightful to look at, and that it was
desirable for obtaining wisdom. So she took some of its fruit and ate it;
she also gave some to her husband, who was with her, and he ate it.

(Genesis 3:1–6)

In their rebellion, human beings claimed the right to act independently of God—to *"be like God"* on their own terms rather than according to His plan. After this, life on earth immediately began to fall
apart. With their disobedience, in which they betrayed their Creator-
King and chose death over life, Adam and Eve forfeited their delegated
rule on earth to Satan (see, for example, Genesis 3:13–19; John 12:31;
Ephesians 2:1–2), and the human race became slaves to rebellion and sin
(see, for example, Romans 6:16). Even the state of nature changed (see
Genesis 3:16–19), with the entire creation coming under bondage due to
the fall of humanity (see Romans 8:19–23). Most significantly, the great
cosmic robbery (with humanity's collusion) caused human beings to lose
their continuous communion with God's Spirit. Ever since then, people
have been looking for a center, a place to restart, a mooring to which their
destiny could be tied.

> The great cosmic robbery postponed the full expression
> of God's Kingdom on earth.

Thus, the robbery postponed the full manifestation and expression
of God's Kingdom on earth. Meanwhile, the whole project seemed like a
failure, and Satan appeared to have achieved his goal of thwarting God's
purposes.

As the old saying goes:

This world had a wonderful beginning,
Man ruined his chances by sinning.

They say that the story will end in God's glory
But at present, the other side seems to be winning!

Every person who has ever lived has been negatively affected by the great cosmic robbery. Every culture that has ever existed has been weakened and broken by this devastating event. No war or series of wars has ever damaged the totality of society as this shocking loss has. And the beat has gone on, century after century, in what appears to be an unending struggle between kingdoms, one of light, the other of darkness. In fact, the general theme of the Old Testament seems to be "sin's sad story." And what we see today, thousands of years down the line, is the continuation of that sad trail, which, as I expressed earlier, has led to seemingly greater devastation and confusion than ever.

If we were to judge by appearances and the sheer statistics of the world's social, economic, and political ills, it would look like an unwinnable war for the Kingdom of light, except for one consideration: the Creator-King always consummates what He initiates. The real, complete, and powerful eternal Kingdom endures! From the beginning, God had a Kingdom in mind for earth as it is in heaven. The devil had a counter idea, but God is God—and He always wins. God will fulfill His *cosmic initiative*.

A Type of the Kingdom on Earth

Ever since the fall of humanity, God has persistently pursued His purpose to redeem humankind and to restore our participation in His Kingdom rule in the world. The biblical record of God's ongoing relationship with humanity as a whole and with individual human beings is a fascinating narrative of this Kingdom project.

During the thousands of years between the fall of humanity and the renewal of the Kingdom on earth through Jesus Christ, God established a type, or pattern, of the eternal Kingdom in the form of the nation of Israel. The Israelites were God's people, and they were to be a reflection of the Kingdom on earth and a witness to the other nations of its reality. Yet the Israelites failed to live up to their high calling. They, too, consistently rebelled against their Creator-King.

The book of Malachi the prophet vividly describes the devastating impact of the great cosmic robbery as it was reflected in the rebellion of the nation of Israel. Some of the last verses of the Old Testament are a prophetic word from God that sums up the situation while presenting the offer of an alternative:

> *Look, I am going to send you Elijah the prophet before the great and awesome Day of the* LORD *comes. And He will turn the hearts of fathers to their children and the hearts of children to their fathers. Otherwise, I will come and strike the land with a curse.* (Malachi 4:5–6)

Following this word, there began one of the most noteworthy periods of recorded history, namely, the four-hundred-year period of heavenly silence between God's prophecy to Malachi and His New Testament announcement of the arrival of Jesus the Messiah. As far as we know, there was not one word of revelation from God during that time.

It is impossible to imagine what kind of season this long stretch of silence must have been for God's people. All they had to go on, as far as fresh revelation from heaven, was what had been spoken the last time they had received a communication from God—which, for the most part, seemed rather bereft of hope. Where God was and what He was doing must have seemed a mystery to them.

Let us review this "last letter from God" to Israel through Malachi, as well as its historical context, to better understand the very next word He spoke four centuries later. The prophet's burden of responsibility was not a pleasant one. The nation of Israel was doubtlessly in a terrible mess when Malachi wrote his book. The people had to be confronted with their rebellion against God, their refusal to keep covenant with Him, and their absolute failure to achieve anything that looked like stability, much less a true reflection of almighty God.

Although the early verses of God's message through Malachi were encouraging, about the only thing that would have been clear was that God was not entirely through with Project Earth in general and with Israel in particular. It begins with the Lord saying, *"I have loved you"* (Malachi 1:2). However, the people reply with skeptical inquiry, not with devotion and obedience, as they ask, *"How have You loved us?"* (verse 2). This is a statement of disbelief, their essential problem. It is a clear sign that the people being addressed had lost their way.

Then God declares to the priests, "You have despised My name." (See Malachi 1:6.) Again, they plead ignorance and ask, *"How have we despised Your name?"* (verse 6). In chapters 1–3 of Malachi, the same sequence of statements and questions is repeated: (1) God outlines the problem; (2) the people protest, *"How...?"*; and (3) God obliges the people's question, cataloging their sin in His answer. The following is a summary of the ways in which the Israelites had disobeyed God.

+ Defective Worship/Profaning God's Table

The people were offering unacceptable sacrifices of lame and sick animals (and the priests were going along with it), and keeping the best for themselves, so their sacrifices had no value. (See Malachi 1:6–14.)

+ Complaining

Added to their sin of profaning God's table was their whining about God's unresponsiveness, even as they disobeyed Him. (See Malachi 2:13–16.)

+ Wearying God

The people wearied God by saying, *"Everyone who does what is evil is good in the LORD's sight, and He is pleased with them"* (Malachi 2:17).

+ Robbery and Theft

The cloud of the people's offenses darkens further with the declaration that they had robbed God by withholding tithes and offerings; apparently, greed was rampant among them. (See Malachi 3:7–12.)

+ Harsh Words Toward God

The Lord tells the people, in effect, "You have said, 'It is useless to serve God; we have gained nothing by keeping His requirements. The arrogant are fortunate. Those who commit wickedness prosper; they test God and escape.'" The Israelites had rejected God's Word and were maligning His reputation as their Provider and Protector. (See Malachi 3:14–15.)

Then, suddenly, both God's mood and His mode seem to change. His fierce words are mixed with promised blessing:

> At that time those who feared the LORD spoke to one another. The LORD took notice and listened. So a book of remembrance was written before Him for those who feared Yahweh [the LORD] and had high regard for His name. "They will be Mine," says the LORD of Hosts, "a special possession on the day I am preparing. I will have compassion on them as a man has compassion on his son who serves him. So you will again see the difference between the righteous and the wicked, between one who serves God and one who does not serve Him."
>
> (Malachi 3:16–18)

A scathing report of future justice opens the final chapter of Malachi:

> "For indeed, the day is coming, burning like a furnace, when all the arrogant and everyone who commits wickedness will become stubble. The coming day will consume them," says the LORD of Hosts, "not leaving them root or branches." (Malachi 4:1)

After that grim statement, which is a powerful assessment of the severity of coming judgment, as well as a declaration that God is still in business, the Lord pronounces both a fearful threat and a glorious promise of future things. Let's look again at the last verses of Malachi:

> Remember the instruction of Moses My servant, the statutes and ordinances I commanded him at Horeb for all Israel. Look, I am going to send you Elijah the prophet before the great and awesome Day of the LORD comes. And he will turn the hearts of fathers to their children and the hearts of the children to their fathers. Otherwise, I will come and strike the land with a curse. (Malachi 4:4–6)

It is worth noting that the last word of the Old Testament is *"curse"*— the seventh time the word *"curse"* or *"cursed"* is used in Malachi. The effects of the great cosmic robbery continued to manifest on earth in the ongoing rebellion of humanity, as well as in creation's bondage due to sin. In contrast, the nature of the Kingdom, as Paul taught, is *"righteousness, peace, and joy in the Holy Spirit"* (Romans 14:17).

The Solution to the Cosmic Robbery

Fast-forward four hundred years, to the time when Jesus was born. We will now look further into the Malachi prophecy in light of New Testament realities. Both Jesus and John the Baptist—who announced the Messiah's arrival and prepared the Israelites for it—were referred to in God's message to Malachi:

> *See, I am going to send My messenger* [John the Baptist], *and he will clear the way before Me. Then the Lord* [Jesus] *you seek will suddenly come to His temple, the Messenger* [Jesus] *of the covenant you desire—see, He is coming," says the* LORD *of Hosts. But who can endure the day of His coming? And who will be able to stand when He appears?*   (Malachi 3:1–2)

God broke His four-hundred-year silence not just with a new prophetic word but by sending *the* Word—the Son of God—to earth with the message of the Kingdom! (Interestingly, the conditions at that time seem to resemble ours in century twenty-one.) The message and manifestation of the Kingdom, apparently absent for centuries, were back on track. In the person of Jesus Christ, they were about to make a cosmic impact on the universe.

> *In the person of Jesus Christ,*
> *the message and manifestation of the Kingdom*
> *were about to make a cosmic impact.*

The Bible gives a number of details about Jesus' miraculous, divine birth. However, with one exception, it does not record anything about Him or from Him for approximately the first thirty years of His life. That one exception is recorded in Luke 2:41–52. Allow me to summarize this account.

Jesus and His earthly parents, Mary and Joseph, had attended the annual Passover festival in Jerusalem, which was about sixty-five miles from their home in Nazareth. Traveling that distance by foot would take several days, and large groups of relatives and friends would often journey together. That year, when the festival was over, Jesus' parents left for home, believing that Jesus was on the road with the group, perhaps visiting with extended family or friends. Yet He had stayed behind in Jerusalem without their knowledge. After traveling a full day, they realized He wasn't there, so they returned to Jerusalem to look for Him, finally finding Him in the temple complex, listening and talking to the religious teachers. The Scriptures say, *"All those who heard Him were astounded at His understanding and His answers"* (Luke 2:47).

Mary and Joseph were probably "astounded" in a different way—more like with shock, anxiety, and anger. When Jesus' mother asked Him why He had stayed behind without telling them, it was most assuredly not a kind, casual inquiry! *"Son, why have You treated us like this? Your father and I have been anxiously searching for You"* (Luke 2:48). Jesus' response was both kind and calm: *"Why were you searching for Me?"* He asked them. *"Didn't you know that I had to be in My Father's house?"* (Luke 2:49). Some other Bible versions translate the last part of this verse as *"…be about My Father's business?"* (See, for example, NKJV, KJV.)

I want to point out two remarkable things about this account, besides the fact that it is the first report about Jesus' life since the days surrounding His birth: (1) At twelve years of age, He was aware of both His identity and His mission on earth. (2) The Bible says nothing else about His life for eighteen years after this incident. Though we don't know much about Jesus' early life, it is clear from this account that Jesus, God's Messenger, was here to do His *"Father's business"*—and that business was the Kingdom.

The biblical record of Jesus' ministry, with all its miracles, is just a smattering of all He achieved in a little more than three years. The disciple

John, writing in his gospel, makes a sweeping and overwhelming statement about Jesus' accomplishments during that brief time:

> *And there are also many other things that Jesus did, which, if they were written one by one, I suppose not even the world itself could contain the books that would be written.* (John 21:25)

Despite Jesus' demonstration of God's love and forgiveness, and the miracles He performed, such as feeding the multitudes, healing the sick, and even raising the dead, He was crucified by the religious leaders of His day, in conjunction with the Roman government. Yet one of the remarkable things about what seemed to be a most dismal failure in crucifixion—followed by heaven's powerful response of resurrection—is that it all turned out to be God's *magnum opus*, His eternal masterpiece to redeem humanity and restore the Kingdom on earth. I can't explain it, nor can you; and we shouldn't even try. As N. T. Wright expressed, Jesus was a "very odd sort of King."[3] He was willing to look, for all practical purposes, like a loser. He was a Friend to the "wrong" kinds of people—prostitutes, tax collectors, and other sinners, including you and me. In fact, He allowed it all to look like a colossal failure, even though He knew who He was, what His purpose in life was, and what divine authority was in His possession. He suffered His way to wholeness, lost His way to winning, and died His way to life, thus bringing back to this earth the expression of the eternal enterprise of the Kingdom of God.

On the cross, Jesus was victorious over the great cosmic robbery. He defeated the power of sin, death, and Satan on our behalf, and He was raised to life again, in the power of the Holy Spirit, with a new and glorified body. (See, for example, Romans 8:11; Philippians 3:21.) He thereby provided a way for human beings to be restored to their relationship with the Father, enter into new life in Him, and regain their ability to rule under His authority to manifest the Kingdom on earth. Significantly, before Jesus returned to the Father in heaven, He spent forty days teaching His disciples about the Kingdom of God. (See Acts 1:3.) The Kingdom continued to His primary message, even after His resurrection.

---

3. See N. T. Wright, *Simply Jesus* (New York: HarperOne, 2011), chapter 1.

Stage Two of the Cosmic Robbery and Its Effects

When Jesus ascended to heaven, He left a body of people on earth called the church—in Greek *ecclesia*, "the called out" ones—comprised of all who believed in Him. They were empowered by the Holy Spirit to carry out the work of the Kingdom of God in the world. Through them, God released many miraculous manifestations of the Kingdom, and great numbers of people became followers of Christ.

The church that had been founded by Jesus, born in the fires of Pentecost, flamed up for a short while. However, before the end of the century of its formation, it exhibited a downward trend. Why? The second phase of the great cosmic robbery occurred, which was a gradual dilution of the Kingdom gospel message that had, at the beginning, been joyfully understood and proclaimed by Jesus' followers. Once again, the theft was orchestrated by Satan and his kingdom of darkness in order to undermine the purposes of God by deceiving the church and weakening its effectiveness.

In the centuries since, much of the church has lived and proclaimed a truncated form of the gospel—and many believers still do today. In essence, *the church has lost its Kingdom mentality and thus its Kingdom theology and practice.* Recently, a leading church in America was penetrated by thieves who netted six hundred thousand dollars in one night. But compared to the magnitude of the deception and theft we are discussing, that was a mere pittance.

Seven hundred years before Jesus was born, He had been the subject of a wonderful Kingdom announcement:

> For a child will be born for us, a son will be given to us, and the government will be on His shoulders. He will be named Wonderful Counselor, Mighty God, Eternal Father, Prince of Peace. The dominion will be vast, and its prosperity will never end. He will reign on the throne of David and over his Kingdom, to establish and sustain it with justice and righteousness from now on and forever. The zeal of the LORD of Hosts will accomplish this.   (Isaiah 9:6–7)

This was God's great promise of the reign of His Kingdom government on earth. The promise remains true, but it has proven to be a promise detained. I believe this announcement was God's greatest declaration since the one He spoke in the garden of Eden regarding the creation and purpose of humanity:

> Let Us make man in Our image, according to Our likeness. They will rule the fish of the sea, the birds of the sky, the livestock, all the earth, and the creatures that crawl on the earth.   (Genesis 1:26)

Together, these declarations express God's will for the manifestation of His Kingdom on earth, with humanity ruling under the authority of Jesus' government. In a later chapter, "The Kingdom, the Church, and the Gospel," we will explore in more detail the reasons for the loss of the church's Kingdom outlook. Suffice it to say here that the church has settled for an abbreviated version of the gospel that has foreshortened its outlook and limited its power. The full message of the Kingdom life is not being proclaimed, and we have a limited vision of what it means for us to be reconciled to the Father and co-heirs with Jesus Christ.

The Kingdom gospel that Jesus brought to earth is the only message of hope for the world.

Thus, both the church and world have not often seen the reality of God's eternal Kingdom manifested on earth. This is true notwithstanding the biblical record of Jesus' birth, death, and resurrection, and His claims that He was indeed the Messiah from God whose purpose it was to proclaim the good news that the Kingdom had returned to earth and was within reach of us all. As a result, much of the world, wallowing in hopeless misery and crying for someone to make sense of it all, lives as if Jesus had never come.

But Jesus *did* come to earth. He did proclaim and minister the Kingdom gospel, die on a cross, resurrect from the dead, and return to heaven—defeating sin, death, and Satan, and renewing the Kingdom in the world. Upon His arrival in heaven, He was seated at the right hand of His Father's throne. (See, for example, Ephesians 1:20.) He sent the Holy Spirit to earth as the Executor of the eternal Kingdom of God in the world, working through His church. Yes, God is still present on earth, and He is still in business!

Throughout the history of the church, Jesus' Kingdom message has, at times, been recaptured by various believers, churches, and spiritual movements that were able to discern it, but they were not able to sustain this vision. The message and manifestation of the Kingdom of God continues to be subtly stolen by the enemy, by his deliberate and complex plot to keep it hidden.

Nevertheless, the recovery of what was stolen will be just as dramatic and far-reaching as the effects of its long and painful absence. As the gospel of the Kingdom is recovered, its significance will be patently clear. Then it will again become the central message of the church and will be preached until the end of the age. The Kingdom gospel that Jesus brought to earth is the only message of hope for the world, and, for that matter, the entire universe.

It is not likely that we will recover what has been stolen until the church realizes that the robbery has taken place, acknowledges that fact, and seeks to restore a Kingdom mind-set and lifestyle. So, heads up—the greatest theft in history is about to be reversed!

5

THE GREAT COMING RECOVERY

One night, while I was writing this book, the word ALERT appeared on my TV screen, nearly filling it. I quietly hoped for a piece of up-front, wonderful good news. What followed was not even close but rather much more of the same: bad, bad news. I wanted to say, "Is there any good news in the world, in the nations, in the streets, in the homes?" I am firmly convinced that if we are looking for good news on television, we will wind up sadly disappointed.

It doesn't take someone with an Einstein-level brain to recognize that our planet is on a head-on collision course with oblivion, and that the speed with which we are traveling that path seems to be increasing. TV news programs daily chronicle our culture's spiraling morals; meanwhile, angry media interviews and frustration-ignited protests around the nation attempt to make sense of senseless conflicts and tragedies in our social, economic, and political arenas. We seem to have given in to collective insanity. The inmates are running the asylum. These are the inevitable results of the great cosmic robbery.

But enough of the bad news!

Is there any good news from heaven? My glad answer is a resounding, "*Yes!*"

> *This good news of the Kingdom will be proclaimed in all the world as a testimony to all nations. And then the end will come.*
>
> (Matthew 24:14)

There are times when I find myself asking the same question as the writer of Psalm 11: "*When the foundations are being destroyed, what can the righteous do?*" (Psalm 11:3 NIV). This is a great question, and, as far as I am concerned, there is a simple answer to it. The righteous can get on board with God's stated agenda and begin to proclaim the "*good news of the Kingdom,*" which He is once more revealing to the world—a project that is guaranteed by Providence to be completed. Let's explore how.

A Climactic Spiritual Season

The great cosmic robbery, and the resulting loss of the message, mentality, and might of the Kingdom, was devastating for humanity. Yet that loss has been triumphed over by the news that the restoration of all things is coming, through the church's rediscovery of the Kingdom. I believe that we are entering the climactic season, spoken of by Jesus, when the full gospel of the Kingdom will be preached across the earth in the final period of earth's history.

In churches and denominations all over the globe, people hold various positions on eschatology (the study of last things), with some believers advocating either a premillennial, a postmillennial, an amillennial, or another end-time scenario, including various theories on the great tribulation. Personally, I thought I had worked out a perfect end-time theology years ago. But then God hammered the truth of the Kingdom into the middle of my theological framework and freshly demanded, through Jesus, that I "*seek first the Kingdom of God and His righteousness, and all these things will be provided for* [me]." As a result, I have been delightfully delivered from taking sides over issues of eschatology that have divided the body of Christ for years, and I have retreated from "certainties" that the Bible has not fully clarified for us. Instead, I have chosen to focus on the task Jesus has given us—the proclamation of the Kingdom gospel. Could it be that what Jesus told His followers just before His ascension is what He is telling us today?

It is not for you to know times or periods that the Father has set by His own authority. But you will receive power when the Holy Spirit has come on you, and you will be My witnesses in Jerusalem, in all Judea and Samaria, and to the ends of the earth. (Acts 1:7–8)

It is my studied opinion that while the church has been trying to discover in detail what Jesus specifically meant by His various prophetic statements, such as in Matthew 24, we have delayed our realization of the significance of the last part of His reply in that chapter, which appears to be its focus: God wants to use us, in the power of the Holy Spirit, to cover the world with the story of Jesus and the message of His Kingdom.

God wants to use us,

in the power of the Holy Spirit, to cover the

world with the message of His Kingdom.

Additionally, I am aware that a growing number of scholars in the field of eschatology hold the opinion that the events Jesus described in Matthew 24, including the proclamation of the gospel to the world, were fulfilled at the time of the destruction of Jerusalem in 70 AD. I have no protest against this position; Jesus' statements were certainly pertinent and relevant in the first century. However, it is my opinion that the context of many Scriptures, while having relevance for the times in which they were received or written, also have significance for every succeeding age. I am moved very deeply to believe, with much excitement, that Matthew 24:14 is also a promise for the end of the age. Thus, Jesus' statements are an important prophecy of hope for our present days and for those that are coming.

The church has experienced—and is currently experiencing (although in a limited way)—an expression of the Kingdom on earth that is connected to time and space, matter, visibility, and human understanding. However, the "now" will soon give way to the "not yet." We will see the final harvest of souls, the collapse of nations all over the world, and the kingdoms of this world, at last, become the Kingdom of our Lord and of His Christ. (See Revelation 11:15.) The entire system of human kingdoms will be no more, and God's eternal rule will encompass the whole of reality in His limitless, sovereign rule in the new heavens and the new earth. (See Isaiah 65:17; 66:22; 2 Peter 3:13.) It will be the same Kingdom, and the same King, but all created things will be made new. With us as His *"kings and priests"* (Revelation 1:6 NKJV; Revelation 5:10 NKJV), Jesus will reign over the vast cosmos, and His Kingdom will unfold its infinite mysteries forever and ever. The eternal God and His eternal family will rule over the renewed and rapidly-expanding universe. For this we were created, and for this we were redeemed.

Our proclamation of these anticipated events is bound to lead to the spiritual awakening that will prompt the final harvest and bring us into the fullness of all that is eternal. Such thoughts should cause us to stand overwhelmed and breathless before the Mighty God who rules over all. Therefore, no matter what our views on eschatology, and no matter how bad things become in the world before Christ returns, we must have as a primary consideration this vital declaration from our Lord:

> *This good news of the Kingdom will be proclaimed in all the world as a testimony to all nations. And then the end will come.*
>
> (Matthew 24:14)

This one great, strategic accomplishment must first come to pass before the culmination of all things. We can confidently count on this fact: the gospel of Jesus Christ, who is the Kingdom personified, will be preached throughout the world to every nation and ethnic group, in every village and city, on every island and continent, before the end of time. Every human being on the planet, old and young, rich and poor, ruler and ruled, educated and illiterate, will be privy to sufficient information to know Jesus, the King of Kings. Only then can—and will—the end come. This is God's firm word from the lips of none other than His own Son.

Such a declaration must be examined, believed, and applied by all Christians. No system of study regarding the future is complete without an investigation of this great promise. Significantly, the powerful engine that will drive this gospel proclamation is that of the might, message, and mentality of the Kingdom of God.

The Good News of the Kingdom

Let me express what will shortly happen in as clear an announcement as I can make:

> At this present, throbbing moment, God is about to re-reveal to the church throughout the world the good news of His Kingdom!

Do we really understand and accept this reality? There is extraordinarily *good news* for our earth. It is the good news of the Kingdom, and the world must hear it. This is not only a vital issue for the future of all people and the future of all things, but is also a pivotal promise that should color the whole landscape of our thinking now. Our regret over the near loss of the Kingdom message on earth should be replaced by the eternal gladness of the coming worldwide awakening to the gospel. And we need not wait for the fullness of the recovery for our joy to be released. Like Jesus' disciples, we are not encouraged to seek to know when this *"end"* will come. However, every thought process in which we engage should be informed by the one, indispensable fact of the proclamation of the good news throughout the world. And we each have a vital role in this proclamation.

> *The Kingdom has come, the Kingdom is coming,*
> *and the Kingdom will come!*

As I will describe in more detail later in this book, the beginnings of this fulfillment are being accompanied by a worldwide shaking, which seems to be nearing peak expression right now, with many of the institutions, governments, and nations of our world spinning, rumbling, trembling, and falling. I do not know exactly what will occur as the Kingdom gospel is proclaimed, but whatever it is, it is sure to change the face of our ruined and fallen culture and cooperate with God in exalting Jesus Christ—who, in turn, will draw all people to Himself. (See John 12:32.)

All this will occur as the church awakens more fully to its true identity and purpose in the Kingdom. So before you succumb to the relentlessly depressing news that the world is surely going to hell in a handbasket, I have the delightful privilege of telling you that the Kingdom has come, the Kingdom is coming, and the Kingdom will come! Even now, the gospel of the Kingdom is being preached throughout our sin-soaked world with greater anointing, is being heard with greater clarity, and is being received with greater readiness than our generation can remember. And, as the familiar adage goes, "You ain't seen nothing yet!"

Though this awakening will soon spread to the world and touch not only every person but every nation, government, community, and church, it will initially be hidden in plain sight from most people because it is completely spiritual. Only the spiritually perceptive will be aware of its dawning. In light of the above, we as the church must be prepared to recognize and receive the revelation of the Kingdom and to participate in God's unfolding purposes.

Are We Prepared for the Coming Awakening?

One way we can prepare for the coming awakening is to look at the context in which Jesus gave His promise about the proclamation of the Kingdom gospel, which is found in chapters 23 and 24 of Matthew. Jesus began by focusing on the spiritual state of the religious experts—the scribes and the Pharisees—who believed they were doing God's will and were spiritually safe due to their religious knowledge and practices. They never considered the fact that they might be off track, contributing to the problems of the day, or being a spiritual stumbling block to their fellow Israelites.

During Jesus' ministry, there was often nothing but conflict and opposition between our Lord and these two groups, who appear to have been the personification of irritation, confrontation, and stubbornness. Yet the particular encounter in Matthew 23, in which Jesus announced various "woes," is the fiercest such conflict recorded in the New Testament.

It is significant that Jesus' greatest judgments were declared against those who were spiritually self-satisfied—something we should take to heart. All of us in Jesus' audience today who read His words would do well to consider if we have, to any degree, any of the qualities of the scribes and Pharisees that Jesus indicted. If so, we need to repent immediately so we can be reconciled to God and fully participate in the restoration of the Kingdom mind-set, as well as the Kingdom awakening.

Let's look at Jesus' preliminary indictments of the scribes and Pharisees, followed by His list of "woes." A little more background about these groups will help us to better understand Jesus' statements. The scribes seem to have been the "bean-counter" watchdogs, if you please, who brought their findings to the Pharisees, who then enacted them upon their constituents. Thus, the scribes were apparently the strategists, providing information, while the Pharisees were the religious activists who sought to enforce their agendas on the people. Whatever the arrangements or job descriptions, according to Jesus, these two groups sat in the *"chair of Moses,"* from which they exerted a wide influence on the Jewish community. (See Matthew 23:1–4.)

Jesus' words were definite, distinct, and stinging. There is no way to interpret them apart from absolute, open confrontation. He denounced the scribes and Pharisees for the following:

+ They didn't practice what they preached. (See Matthew 23:3.)

+ They loaded the people with heavy burdens—that is, the baggage of man-made religious traditions and practices. (See Matthew 23:4.)

+ They refused to lift a finger to lighten that load. (See Matthew 23:4.)

- ✦ Their primary motivation for their actions was to be noticed by others. (See Matthew 23:5.)

- ✦ They enlarged and lengthened their "badges" of devotion, their phylacteries and tassels, thereby broadcasting their religious superiority. (See Matthew 23:5.)

- ✦ They loved the places of honor at banquets, the front seats in the synagogues, the greetings in the marketplaces, and the privilege of being called "rabbi." (See Matthew 23:7.)

Jesus next pronounced eight specific "woes" upon the religious structures of the day and their promoters. (See Matthew 23:13–16, 23–36.) Before we turn to the actual woes, let's define the word *woe* in this context. A woe is a warning or a rebuke directed toward a person or group for an unrighteous position, attitude, or action that, unless repented of, will lead to judgment. Jesus seems to use the term as a most serious proclamation to warn those who were living in deception and hypocrisy, and who are oppressing others while appearing (or even believing) to be serving God.

Here are the attitudes and actions of the scribes and Pharisees that led Jesus to declare the eight "woes":

Woe one: They inhibited people's entry into God's Kingdom by "locking" it up from them. They themselves didn't go in, nor did they encourage or allow others to go in. (See Matthew 23:13.)

Woe two: They "*devour*[ed] *widows' houses and* [made] *long prayers just for show*" (Matthew 23:14).

Woe three: They traveled far and wide to make proselytes, and by the time they had finished with them, they had made these converts twice as fit for hell as they were. (See Matthew 23:15.)

Woe four: They had taught the people carelessly about making oaths, misunderstanding the holy nature of the altar, the sanctuary, and heaven itself. For example, they said that making an oath by the gold of the temple in Jerusalem was binding, but making an oath by the temple itself was not. Yet Jesus emphasized that making an oath by the temple or by heaven was the same as making an oath by God Himself. (See Matthew 23:16.) Carelessly making an oath by the temple or by heaven was a serious violation. One of the commandments God gave the Israelites was, *"Do not misuse the name of the* LORD *your God, because the* LORD *will not leave anyone unpunished who misuses His name"* (Exodus 20:7; Deuteronomy 5:11).

Woe five: They paid a tenth (a tithe) of their commodities but left unattended *"the weightier matters of the law: justice and mercy and faith"* (Matthew 23:23 NKJV).

Woe six: They were careful to clean the outside of the temple dishes, but their own hearts were *"full of greed and self-indulgence."* Jesus provided the moral to the story: first clean the inside (heart) and then the outside (body) will be clean. (See Matthew 23:25–26.)

Woe seven: They were like whitewashed tombs—beautiful on the outside, but inside full of the bones of their victims and of every impurity. (See Matthew 23:27.)

Woe eight: They rejected the message of God through Jesus (and subsequently His followers) while claiming they would never have rejected and killed the Lord's prophets the way their ancestors did. General hypocrisy is the blight of the religious pretender. Their practice of their religion was fraudulent, and they would receive the judgments to come. (See Matthew 23:29–37.)

After this scorching denunciation of the practices of the scribes and Pharisees, Jesus predicted the destruction of the temple in Jerusalem. When His disciples asked Him when this would occur, and how they would recognize the end of the age, He described the following events, which are a veritable catalog of chaos: the coming of false christs, deception, wars and rumors of wars, famines, and earthquakes. And this was only the beginning! (See Matthew 24:4–8.)

He then announced an impending set of ominous oppressions and turmoil that included persecution of His followers; people taking offense and betraying and hating each other; more false prophets and deception; multiplied lawlessness; and the love of many people growing cold. (See Matthew 24:4–12.)

Then, as if taking a deep breath following the tragic announcement of this looming, deep devastation, Jesus made this stunning declaration:

> *This good news of the Kingdom will be proclaimed in all the world as a testimony to all nations. And then the end will come.*
>
> (Matthew 24:14)

In Matthew 24, Jesus may have been describing events that occurred at the destruction of Jerusalem. (Also note that the conditions depicted there have been duplicated many times in successive centuries.) However, in my mind, there is nothing in that position that would prohibit the belief that we are seeing today the beginnings of the ultimate fulfillment of that word. That means the preaching of the gospel of the Kingdom to the whole world is a living promise in this twenty-first century in which we live! Our part is to prepare our minds to receive the Kingdom mentality, our hearts to embrace Kingdom living, and our lives to receive Kingdom power in the Holy Spirit to transform our culture.

What Gospel Will Be Preached?

To further understand the great coming recovery, let us explore the meaning of Jesus' declaration in Matthew 24:14. This Scripture is often taken to mean, specifically, that the message of salvation through Jesus Christ will be preached to the whole world. However, the verse leaves no doubt as to the full content of the message that will be preached to all nations. Can you fathom the meaning of this simple statement? I suggest you spend a minute just repeating this declaration: *"This good news of the Kingdom will be proclaimed in all the world as a testimony to all nations. And then the end will come."* Repeat it until it stands in the foremost place of your mind as a treasured truth that will impact all your present circumstances and all your tomorrows.

Notice that it is the gospel of the *Kingdom*, not just the gospel of the atonement, that is to be preached. This gospel is about the sovereign rule of God's eternal realm, which is a perfect reflection of His nature and will, and which will be manifested on earth as it is in heaven. The fulfillment of this declaration is going to happen—really, absolutely, guaranteed!

Although the content of the message that is about to cover the world is the good news of the Kingdom, the truths of the substitutionary death of Jesus on the cross and His glorious resurrection are absolutely indispensable within that larger message. They are the means by which we enter the Kingdom in the first place, and they are the means through which we receive the power that enables us to live the Kingdom life. The gospel is *"God's power for salvation to everyone who believes"* (Romans 1:16 NIV). In brief, the preaching of the whole (the Kingdom gospel) will inevitably include this essential part (the gospel of atonement and salvation).

What is the character of God's Kingdom, which is being recovered? In the New Testament, Jesus described God's Kingdom in various ways. For example, when He first began His ministry, He quoted from Isaiah 61, saying,

> *The Spirit of the Lord is on Me, because He has anointed Me to preach good news to the poor. He has sent Me to proclaim freedom to the captives and recovery of sight to the blind, to set free the oppressed, to proclaim the year of the Lord's favor.* (Luke 4:18–19)

In another instance, Jesus said, *"If I drive out demons by the Spirit of God, then the Kingdom of God has come to you"* (Matthew 12:28; see also Luke 11:20). The good news of the Kingdom is that God offers us a life of forgiveness, freedom, grace, power, and purpose!

At this point in our discussion, I ask you to pause from your reading to glimpse at the headlines of a newspaper or an Internet news site, or to remember a line you recently heard in a TV newscast that forecasted the imminent collapse of a community, an institution, a nation, or even the world. Then repeat Matthew 24:14 in the face of all the shocking affairs of today's world. Do you sense any difference in how you think and feel about the news? If not, try another exercise. Recall images you've seen of violence and chaos in the Middle East, such as pillaging, Christians martyred for their faith, multiple beheadings of innocents, and so on. Now repeat the Scripture text again, a bit louder than before, fully aware of God's presence:

> *This good news of the Kingdom will be proclaimed in all the world as a testimony to all nations. And then the end will come.*

Make it a habit to refer to this verse and to repeat it aloud every time you are reminded of the epidemic of tragedy and violence on the earth. It will make a difference in how you think about the world and your role in it. At this moment, God is preparing the church for her greatest days. The good news of the Kingdom will precipitate spiritual awakening, first among those who discover and declare it, then among those who see, hear, and believe it. The awakening will then break out into the end-time harvest.

The Promise and Potential of Awakening

The following are two avenues through which this all-important Kingdom gospel will be communicated to the world for the end-time harvest: (1) by the sounds of those who will preach the simple truths about God's eternal Kingdom, and (2) by the sights of multiplied thousands of men, women, and children who will embody the Kingdom gospel, their lives demonstrating this gospel as they point to Jesus the King.

The very existence of these sights and sounds will mean that many people's hearts will have already been touched by, and their lives surrendered to, the Lord of the Kingdom. Can you imagine the scenes as thousands of people of all ages speak about the Kingdom wherever they go? The exercise of the mammoth task of encircling the globe with the Kingdom gospel will spark spiritual revival as the glorious presence of the King and His Kingdom manifestations are experienced throughout the world.

I do not wish to disparage any spiritual event that occurred in the past and resulted in people coming to Christ, but this soon-approaching harvest will be beyond any experience the earth has witnessed since Pentecost. Likewise, I welcome spiritual revivals on any level, but no previous awakening has been perfect or lasting. Though they have burned brightly for a while, many, if not most, have died down all too soon—the flames being reduced to cooling embers and finally cold ashes. Again, a few of these awakenings have discovered the reality of the Kingdom and have held on to it for a time; consequently, they have burned more brightly and for a longer period, but all have eventually waned and become only memories.

But this final awakening? The Kingdom will be preached worldwide, God's name will be honored, the Holy Spirit's power will be released, and Jesus Christ will be exalted and adored; then, as previously expressed, He will draw people to Himself, as He promised. (See John 12:32.)

Let's read Jesus' declaration once again:

This good news of the Kingdom will be proclaimed in all the world as a testimony to all nations. And then the end will come.

(Matthew 24:14)

Jesus' statement includes the words, "*in all the world as a testimony to all nations.*" All nations—that means from Afghanistan and Albania to Zambia and Zimbabwe! Every metropolis, city, town, village, and wide spot in the road will be the scene of a holy conflagration and powerful visitation.

> *The final Kingdom harvest will be beyond any the earth has witnessed since Pentecost.*

Here is how I envision the great harvest: imagine every spiritual awakening in history being thrown together as logs on the fire. The message of the Kingdom will be proclaimed by Spirit-anointed believers everywhere, and the name of Jesus will be on people's lips in all nations. Schoolrooms will become places of Kingdom instruction. Choruses and hymns of praise will resound throughout the streets and neighborhoods. The sounds of this music will be interrupted at times by the blood-curdling screams of those who are being delivered from demons to be joyfully set free.

No sooner will the news media chronicle a tidal wave of the Spirit in one nation than another will break out in another country. Cultures previously bound in anti-Christian persecution—those that terrified, tortured, and murdered believers—will witness Kingdom manifestations as thousands of people rush to trust Jesus Christ as Savior and Lord.

People's time-honored traditions will be abandoned and daily routines will be shattered. Governments will be in a state of confusion, and officials will be forced to cease their normal endeavors. Wall Street will be silent and empty because all the excitement and "business" will be elsewhere. Highways will be so crowded by seekers that commerce will be interrupted. No professional athletic contests will be held; sports stadiums, filled to capacity, will become scenes of Kingdom happenings, including healings and miracles. The sick will be carried by emergency vehicles to locations where the blind are receiving their sight and the paralyzed are standing up, walking, and running.

Military bases all over the world will be assaulted in a spiritual way, with many servicemen and women coming to Christ. Seaports and airports will become dramatic scenes where crews and passengers of ships coming into port and planes touching down on the runway will tell of sudden spiritual events that changed the whole atmosphere on board as soon as they caught sight of land. Resurrections will be witnessed and widely reported. This will occur everywhere! Holy pandemonium will reign, because good news travels fast!

News feeds will continue to report over a rapidly-widening area of the world, until this remarkable visitation is heralded in every country. As these things are being reported in the news, crowds will show up at television and radio stations. Many people will be weeping in fear and panic, while others will be shouting with joy. Helplessly trembling, many will blurt out questions like, "What is this?" "What is going on?" "What I must I do to know this Christ?"

Nightfall will bring no letup to the spontaneous gatherings of thousands of people of all racial, ethnic, and socioeconomic backgrounds, and geographical areas. Yet even in the midst of all the excitement and rising panic, there will seem to come over the crowds a certain calm, allowing people to give testimonies of Kingdom visions, revelations, and miracles. Accordingly, as groups of worshipping, weeping people come together, someone in the group will ask for silence to allow an explanation for all that is happening. Excited conversations will burst forth as people blurt out, "I just found God!" or "I've just been healed!" or "Jesus appeared to me!" The sun will rise on the multitude of groups excitedly discussing the night's events. Church leaders will rush to open their buildings and welcome the crowds. People will say, "What should we do to be saved?" and "This is God's doing; there is no other explanation!"

Do you think I have overstated this issue? Well, pardon me, but I have not yet begun to describe the glory days of this planet's future! What God has in store for us is beyond description; it is elevated above our imaginations. I have not even touched on the size of His plans, as this verse from Paul expresses:

> But as it is written: What eye did not see and ear did not hear, and what never entered the human mind—God prepared this for those who love Him. (1 Corinthians 2:9)

I hear the voices of those who protest, "You have taken this verse out of context; and besides, what you have described is not part of my eschatological calendar of end-time events!" As I expressed earlier, I believe that regardless of the contextual implications, there are certain Scriptures that are applicable and significant for our situations today, including the one above. If your eschatology distresses and depresses you, I question the direction of your theology. More than any of us, God knows what is in store for the earth, and He is neither depressed nor defeated by world conditions today or by anything that will occur in the future. (See, for example, Psalm 2:1–12.) Therefore, I counsel you to change your perspective, revise your eschatological calendar, and rejoice!

The best word I can think of to anchor my certainty regarding the recovery of what was stolen in the great cosmic robbery is *inexorable*. This word refers to something that is inevitable, pending, bound to happen, completely unavoidable, absolutely beyond the realm of being stopped. The message and mentality of the Kingdom of God will be recovered, restored, and re-demonstrated—and it is starting to happen already.

The Knowledge and Glory of the Lord

I have previously emphasized that developing a Kingdom mind-set that will allow us to participate in this recovery involves committing to a process of renewing our minds and hearts. Therefore, I want to give you some additional encouragement in this process. In my opinion, the best book in the Bible for examining the promise and potential of awakening is Habakkuk. The prophet Habakkuk did not see the revival that he prayed for in his time, but he learned to wait for God's time. We must be willing to do the same and we grow in our understanding of the Kingdom life.

It would do you well to read this often-overlooked book, especially since it is only fifty-six verses in length. You can get the drift of it while reading it quickly, and I believe it will help you to put our present world conditions into perspective. In the meantime, let me provide a short summary of the book of Habakkuk.

Habakkuk lived in a day when things weren't going well at all, so he chose to have a talk with the Lord, saying, in effect, "How long do I have to pray before You will listen? Don't You see how bad things are? Do I have to explain it to You? Do You even care? Are you going to do anything about it? (See Habakkuk 1:1–4.)

God replies, "Take a good, long look around you. You haven't seen anything yet! I'm about to turn some really bad armies loose on you. They are mean and nasty and ride fast horses. They are faster than leopards and swifter than eagles swooping for a catch! They mock at kings, laugh at defenders, and take prisoners like sand. They're going to ridicule, steal, and tear things up, and no one on earth can stop them. They worship their own strength, and they are guilty before Me." (See Habakkuk 1:5–11.)

Hearing this, Habakkuk answers, "What are You saying? Aren't you the everlasting God? Aren't you the righteous Judge? You won't stand for this, will You? People getting away with evil, and getting rich in the process? Are You going to let this continue? I'm going to wait and see how You will answer." (See Habakkuk 1:12–2:1.)

God replies to Habakkuk, "My son, I am going to tell you something important, so write it out in large letters in your little notebook, so you can clearly see it. Here it is: I may seem slow, but I'm never late. Everything is working according to My timing. Those who are arrogant and cruel may have big egos, but the hard-headed finish last. Meanwhile, those who are righteous will live by their faith. Evildoers may run over them, and they may hurt for a while. Yet another day is coming, and woe [five woes— count them] to those who abuse and oppress people. Know this: the whole world is going to be filled with My knowledge and glory, as deep and wide as the sea. The idols and false gods that people create for themselves are just gold-plated deadness; they are breathless and lifeless. But I am the living God, and I dwell in My temple—everyone on earth should keep silent before Me." (See Habakkuk 2:2–20.)

> God has never left us. In His timing,
> the good news of the Kingdom will be proclaimed in
> all the earth, and He will be glorified.

Habakkuk then prays, "Lord, I've heard all about You, and I am awe-struck. Remember us in Your mercy. I see You coming to judge the earth, and the whole world praises You. You show Your might like lightning! The wind is blowing, the mountains are falling, the land is trembling, and the oceans are surging. You have come to punish the nations and to save Your people.

"Yes, I've heard of You, God, and I've seen You, and I'm shaking in my boots! Now I'm going to watch and wait for You to deliver us from those who seek to destroy us. The orchard isn't bearing any fruit, the fields are dead, and the sheep and cows are gone. Nevertheless, I will rejoice in God, who makes me strong! He makes me like a nimble deer on a rough mountain path. He helps me to walk on high places." (See Habakkuk 3.)

Thank you, Habakkuk, for recording God's words—I think we've got the message now! God has been here all along. He has never left us, and in His timing, the good news of the Kingdom *will* be proclaimed. The end may be near, but before it comes, the gospel will be preached in all the earth, and God will be glorified.

These may be the worst of times, but I assure you, better times are coming, compliments of the gospel of the Kingdom. Let's get ready! Then, as the song says, "Let earth receive her King!"

6

THE KINGDOM, THE CHURCH, AND THE GOSPEL

I n his incomparable book *The Kingdom: The Emerging Rule of Christ Among Men*, George Dana Boardman states, "Two words [*Kingdom* and *church*] occur in the New Testament so frequently that they largely characterize it, and almost dominate it."[4] For our strategic study here, I have added the word *gospel*. The significance of this third word will become clear as we further explore how the church and the gospel function as parts within the whole of the Kingdom of God.

Please don't skim over this chapter. The relationship between these entities must be clarified and reflected on to counteract three misunderstandings that hang over the twenty-first-century church like a foreboding cloud, obscuring its calling:

1. The near loss of the message and mentality of God's Kingdom as central to our understanding of God and His ways, as well as to our identity and role in His Kingdom purposes. We have discussed this development in the last two chapters.

---

4. George Dana Boardman, *The Kingdom: The Emerging Rule of Christ Among Men* (Shippensburg, PA: Destiny Image Publishers, 2008), 19. Boardman also wrote a second volume on the church, which has been reprinted as *The Church: The Divine Ideal* (Shippensburg, PA: Destiny Image Publishers, 2008).

2. The identification of the Kingdom as synonymous with the church, or the church as synonymous with the Kingdom. Such a misconception blurs the identities of both Kingdom and church, thus lessening the probability that we will receive a full revelation of each. Again, the Kingdom is the whole into which everything else fits. For us to fail to define, declare, and relate to the Kingdom as primary guarantees a degree of failure in carrying out our purpose, even if we have a valid perspective on both the church and the gospel. We must remember that it was only regarding the Kingdom that Jesus commanded, "*Seek first…*" (Matthew 6:33).

> *The concept of the Kingdom has suffered*
> *great neglect in the church because it is thought of as*
> *a later reality that is not fully relevant for today.*

3. The limiting of the Kingdom concept to realities and events in the future, thus overlooking the full Kingdom narrative, with its present expression on earth. The concept and outlook of the Kingdom of God have suffered great neglect in the church because the Kingdom is largely perceived to be a later reality that is not completely relevant for today. The tragedy of this far-off approach is that it leaves the church and thus Christianity both Kingdom-less and powerless. Furthermore, portions of the church have a subtle but keenly-developed sense of denial about the reality and centrality of the Kingdom, due to their frenetic scramble to be "relevant" and "successful" in the eyes of the world.

Yet the eternal Kingdom is relevant for the past, the present, and the future. It was the rule of God in the eternal past; it is the rule of God in the confusing present; and it will be the rule of God in the glorious future—"*and He will reign forever and ever!*" (Revelation 11:15).

It is my conviction that this third misunderstanding, and its corresponding neglect, is the costliest issue in today's church, particularly in the

West. Seeing the Kingdom as solely in the future can rob the church's incentive to holy living. Moreover, when both the presence and the power of the Kingdom are relegated to the future, the church profoundly lacks its foundation of strength to change the existing culture.

These issues can be resolved only by a fresh invasion of Kingdom revelation. Holiness is a commitment issue, but it is often mistaken for a discipline issue. We are not holy by any means as a result of what we do for God; thus, "doing business for God" must not be mistaken for a righteous life. Holiness is an intrinsic part of the nature of God, and no one can be holy without Him. Only total yieldedness to God and His eternal rule will result in a truly holy life. In fact, only as we personally make ourselves completely available to Him on an ongoing basis can we embody this life of holiness. Therefore, the Kingdom of God strongly calls for holiness while, at the same time, it affords us both the incentives and the dynamics to enable us to live holy lives.

As the Kingdom is revealed in its fullness, it also comes with authority in the name of our risen Lord to deal with the evil constructs in the world. Remember that in the days of Jesus' ministry, the frequency of demonic conflict He experienced and His victory over it was such that He used it as undeniable proof that the Kingdom had come, declaring, *"If I drive out demons by the Spirit of God, then the Kingdom of God has come to you"* (Matthew 12:28).

The Kingdom is also what gives the church its significance. E. Stanley Jones, in his signature book, *The Unshakable Kingdom*, observes,

> In both cases, Protestant and Catholic, the attitude of humanity was this: If the Church and the kingdom of God are the same, then the kingdom of God doesn't matter much, for the Church doesn't matter much; it is irrelevant. But suppose the Church takes its true position and points to the Kingdom and its total relevancy, then the Church becomes relevant in the Kingdom's relevancy.[5]

---

5. E. Stanley Jones, *The Unshakable Kingdom and the Unchanging Person* (Bellingham, WA: McNett Press, 1995), 70.

This is a huge observation about how the world, in general, views the church as insignificant, but how a renewed connection to the Kingdom will change that. If this view is correct—and I think it is—it will bring a new day to our participation in both the Kingdom and the church, as well as the gospel that connects them.

It is crucial that we remedy the triple tragedy described above by addressing each of these issues and allowing the Kingdom to take its place in earthly history, as well as in eternity. Until we do this, the church will experience little unity and meager power to advance the interests of God on earth, and will see limited success in transforming the societies of the world. Our expressions of true Christianity will remain deficient in their authority, divided in their doctrines, and diluted in their power to bring transformation.

Strategic Kingdom Meanings

It is difficult to evaluate the significance of some words until they are linked with others. In the case of these three—*Kingdom, church,* and *gospel*—we may consider them important in themselves, but when they are connected, they explode into life-transforming and culture-changing concepts and forces. Thus, when the three great and glorious entities of Kingdom, church, and gospel are illuminated as to their meaning and relationship, and are fitted together in the order God intended, then the foundation of true, lasting spiritual awakening will be laid, and their interrelated dynamics will be manifested. It is my intense hope that clarity and correction on these issues will lead us all to an accurate assessment of God's purposes for the church in the world.

I want to leave you with a fresh view of each of these three concepts, as well as an excitement and expectation for how God will use them in combination, with our involvement. I believe that a careful reading of this chapter, coupled with a serious resolve to make strategic shifts in our thinking and our lives, will prepare us for the rest of the journey.

Before seeking to intermingle these words for maximum effect, let's take each one by itself.

The Kingdom

In the New Testament, the Greek word translated as "Kingdom," *basileia*, appears one hundred and forty times: one hundred and nine times in the Gospels, eight times in Acts, fourteen times in Paul's epistles, twice in Hebrews, once in James, once in 1 Peter, and five times in Revelation.[6] The very first words spoken by John the Baptist in the book of Matthew were an announcement that the Kingdom had *"come near"* (Matthew 3:2), or was *"at hand"* (NKJV, KJV), along with the corresponding necessity of repenting. Jesus' first recorded statements in Matthew and Mark contained exactly the same words (see Matthew 4:17), with the Mark account merely having a different word order, with the additional announcement, *"The time is fulfilled.... Believe in the good news!"* (Mark 1:15).

> *The whole emphasis of Jesus' earthly ministry was the Kingdom of God.*

We have noted that the whole emphasis of Jesus' earthly ministry was the Kingdom of God, which we have defined as His rule both in eternity and in time. In addition to announcing that the Kingdom had *"come near"* on earth, essentially every parable Jesus told was a Kingdom parable, every story a Kingdom story, and every miracle a Kingdom event. Again, after His death and resurrection, He maintained the same theme, holding a forty-day "conference" on the Kingdom for His disciples. (See Acts 1:3.) Shortly after this, He handed off the administration of that Kingdom to the Holy Spirit, whom He personally sent to His disciples to carry out Kingdom business in His place. (See, for example, John 14:26; Acts 1:8.) Paul emphasized this connection between God's Kingdom and God's Spirit when he wrote,

---

6. Boardman, *Kingdom*, 19.

*For the Kingdom of God is not eating and drinking, but righteousness, peace, and joy **in the Holy Spirit**.*　　　　　　　　(Romans 14:17)

The Church

The New Testament word translated as *"church"* is *ecclesia*. *Ecclesia* was a common Greek word in Jesus' day that was used to refer to a gathering of any kind. It literally means "the called out," which is a rather descriptive word for the church, don't you think? In a religious context, it is used one hundred and eleven times in the New Testament: three times in Matthew, twenty times in Acts, sixty-two times in Paul's epistles, twice in Hebrews, once in James, three times in John's third epistle, and twenty times in Revelation.[7]

When the term is used in the New Testament, it refers either to a body of believers in a certain location, such as "the church at Ephesus," or to the invisible, universal entity comprising all who are born again, of whom Christ is the Head: *"For the husband is the head of the wife as Christ is the head of the church. He is the Savior of the body"* (Ephesians 5:23).

The Relationship Between Kingdom and Church

Let us now look at the relationship between the Kingdom of God and the church from two vantage points: first, from human observation; second, directly from the lips of Jesus Himself.

I gladly defer to George Dana Boardman and his priceless coverage of this subject in his book *The Kingdom: The Emerging Rule of Christ Among Men*, which I quoted from earlier. Bob Mumford and I worked together to see that this book, which was first written at the end of the nineteenth century, was republished so that today's believers could benefit from Boardman's insights. His work is so concise and clear, and I am in such complete agreement with him, that in the following paragraphs, I will either directly quote from him or paraphrase his views.

As Boardman points out, *basileia* is used more frequently in the Gospels, whereas *ecclesia* is used more in Acts and the Epistles. He also writes,

---

7. Ibid.

In "Basileia" or "Kingdom" the Divine or Kingly element prevails—it is the Reign Of God; in "Ecclesia" or "Church" the human or social element prevails—it is a congregation of Christians; or to put it in another form: in Basileia Christianity appears as a spiritual organism—"Righteousness, and peace, and joy in the Holy Spirit"; in Ecclesia Christianity appears as an institutional organization—"The Ecclesia which was in Jerusalem."

...Basileia or Kingdom is God's end—the goal of Christianity; Ecclesia or Church is God's means—the method of Christianity. Thus the Kingdom descends in order that the Church may ascend.

...Accordingly as "Kingdom" precedes "Church," both chronologically and logically, our subject naturally cleaves into two parts—the Christian Kingdom and the Christian Church."[8]

Again, I appreciate Boardman's contributions because I believe his book contains the best explanation that I know of regarding the important relationship between the Kingdom and the church.

And now, let us hear from Jesus Himself:

When Jesus came to the region of Caesarea Philippi, He asked His disciples, "Who do people say that the Son of Man is?" And they said, "Some say John the Baptist; others, Elijah; still others, Jeremiah or one of the prophets." "But you," He asked them, "who do you say that I am?" Simon Peter answered, "You are the Messiah, the Son of the living God!" And Jesus responded, "Simon son of Jonah, you are blessed because flesh and blood did not reveal this to you, but My Father in heaven. And I also say to you that you are Peter, and on this rock I will build My **church,** *and the forces of Hades will not overpower it. I will give to you the keys of the* **Kingdom of heaven,** *and whatever you bind on earth is already bound in heaven, and whatever you loose on earth is already loosed in heaven."* (Matthew 16:13–19)

Let us tune in to the thinking of Jesus and determine to plunge into a secret that, I believe, can liberate us to see these epic subjects of the Kingdom, the church, and the gospel not only as they stand alone, but also as they relate

8. Ibid, 20.

to one another. I have openly and repeatedly declared that the Kingdom of God is "everything," that is, the sum total of all reality, the whole that is greater than the sum of its parts. When Jesus came to earth, He brought His Kingdom with Him, which is to say that He came as the Kingdom of God personified. Then He established His church, promising that He would build it, and guaranteed its success. The church is comprised of all who have entered the Kingdom through the doorway of Christ's atoning work. So the church is the whole body of believers who dwell in Christ, their Head. And Christ is the King of the Kingdom, sent from the Father. Thus, there is no competition between the Kingdom and the church. I think of it along these lines:

> The lesser, alone, is incomplete.
> The lesser does not contain the greater, but
> The greater always contains the lesser.

The Gospel

And what about the gospel? Initially, Jesus and His disciples preached the *"good news* [gospel] *about the Kingdom of God,"* or the good news about God's reign—period. (See, for example, Luke 4:43; Acts 8:12.) As we have previously discussed, these days, when we talk about the "gospel," we usually mean the message of salvation in Jesus, or His sacrifice for our sins. But when Jesus died for our sins on the cross and was raised from the dead by the power of God, the gospel of the Kingdom was completed, fulfilled, and crowned.

Does this mean there are two different gospels? No, there is one gospel with two glorious facets! The first facet, the gospel of the Kingdom, is eternal, with no beginning and no end; summed up, it says, "God reigns, and He invites you to live with Him in His Kingdom." The other facet is what we call the gospel of the atonement, the good news of the saving power of the blood of Jesus, which was necessitated by the separation caused by humanity's rebellion against God. God has always reigned, but Jesus Christ died for our rebellion and sin, opening the way for us to enter His Kingdom. We could not enter the Kingdom without receiving what He has done for us. This legal action, enacted by our loving heavenly Father, is what gives us the two-faceted gospel, which includes forgiveness as well as the high privilege of living in the Kingdom family.

> *The complete gospel embraces both*
> *Kingdom and atonement.*

The term "full gospel" was coined during the early days of the charismatic movement as an indication that the life of the Spirit needed to be restored to the church. While the term is not used as frequently today, we might well apply it to our description of the gospel here. The complete gospel embraces both Kingdom and atonement. It presents the suffering and death of Jesus as total satisfaction—propitiation—for the violated holiness of God. It also shows us the joyful face of grace, in which the right is universally granted for every born-again individual to be a citizen of God's Kingdom, with its limitless privileges and mighty power!

I cannot resist including here what I perceive to be the greatest treatise on the gospel of the Kingdom, written by George Dana Boardman. For me, it throbs with life and flows with revelation. First, we behold the seminal statements of Jesus regarding the gospel of the Kingdom:

From that time began Jesus to preach the gospel, evangel, good news of God, and to say, The time is fulfilled, and the Kingdom of God is at hand: repent, and believe in the gospel, the kingdom; I must preach the good news of the kingdom to the other cities also, for therefore was I sent; He went about through cities and villages, bringing the good tidings of the kingdom of God; Jesus went round about all the cities and the villages teaching in their synagogues, and announcing the evangel of the kingdom; this evangel of the kingdom shall be preached in all the

inhabited earth for a testimony to all the nations; and then will come
the end (Matthew 4:23; 9:35; 24:14; Mark 1:14; Luke 8:1, etc.).[9]

Regarding the above Scriptures, Boardman wrote, "No wonder then
that the Kingdom of God is so often spoken of as a divine *evanggelion*,
evangel, glad tidings, good news, gospel."[10]

Let us now read the summation of the clearest declaration of the gospel of the Kingdom:

> Beware, then, of limiting this word "gospel" to what we call
> Christ's "atoning sacrifice." For when our King went about in Gal-
> ilee heralding the gospel of His Kingdom, it was in the early part
> of His ministry, long before He foretold His own passion and
> death; long before His apostles asserted and unfolded the blessed
> doctrine of Christ's reconciling sacrifice. The truth is, the re-en-
> thronement of God in man is in the deepest sense the evangel,
> the good news, the gospel. For the reinstatement of God's domin-
> ion in this insurgent world is the grand and blessed fact of human
> time. To this one supreme end everything else is but instrumental;
> for example, God's Bible is instrumental in way of informing and
> guiding; God's providence is instrumental in way of controlling
> the affairs of men, the march of events, the progress of discoveries;
> God's Spirit is instrumental in way of quickening, illuminating,
> upbuilding; God's Son is instrumental in way of reconciling, rec-
> tifying, saving. Nay, the atonement itself is but a means to an end,
> and this end is the reestablishment of God's empire in man, the
> restoration of God's diadem over mankind, the return of Jehovah
> God to walk again with His children in the garden at the cool
> of the day. God's re-enthronement means man's salvation, even as
> man's salvation means God's re-enthronement. Well, then, may
> this Kingdom of God be called a kingly evangel, a blessed news, a
> royal gospel. To be told that, notwithstanding all our rebellion, the
> Almighty King has not eternally outlawed us; to be assured that,
> notwithstanding all our moral uncleanness, the infinitely shining

---

9. Ibid., 51. Italics are in the original.
10. Ibid.

One is not ashamed to stoop down and resume His sway within us; to be certified that Eternal God in the person of His own Son is yearning to make entry into our guilty, miserable souls, that He may enshrine Himself within us in infinite love and eternal peace—this is indeed a very gospel, ay, it is the gospel itself. If this is not glad tidings, pray tell me what you mean by good news.

> *How beautiful upon the mountains are the feet of Him that brings good tidings, that publishes peace, that brings good tidings of good, that publishes salvation; that says to Zion, THY GOD REIGNS* (Isaiah 52:7).[11]

I have just reread this uplifting declaration of our emancipation, and I recommend that you do the same!

The Dynamics of Kingdom, Church, and Gospel

The Kingdom of God, then, is the reign of God, both in eternity and in time. The Kingdom on earth is manifested by the Holy Spirit as He works through the body of Christ, the church, whose members are co-heirs with the King. Each member is enrolled in what we might call Kingdom University, with a major in "Training for Reigning"—both for here and for the hereafter. The church has also been entrusted with a redeeming narrative called the *gospel* that, once proclaimed, enables others to enter the Kingdom, as well, and to understand the eternal Kingdom they have been invited to enter.

In the following chapter, we will examine in more detail the dynamics of the functional relationship between the Kingdom, the church, and the gospel through "The Keys of the Kingdom."

---

11. Ibid., 51–52.

7

THE KEYS OF THE KINGDOM

The only time in Jesus' earthly ministry that He spoke of both the church and the Kingdom together was in the passage below. That fact, in itself, makes His words both significant and intriguing.

> *On this rock I will build My church, and the forces of Hades will not overpower it. I will give you the keys of the Kingdom of heaven, and whatever you bind on earth is already bound in heaven, and whatever you loose on earth is already loosed in heaven.* (Matthew 16:18–19)

With these words, what is Jesus telling us about the nature of the church?

1. *"I will build [it]"*—Jesus is the Builder of the church.

2. *"My church"*—Jesus is the sole Owner of the church.

3. *"The forces of Hades will not overpower it"*—Jesus' church cannot be stopped even by hell itself.

Let's pause here to consider the powerful and eternal relevance of the following statement by repeating it aloud several times:

> *On this rock I will build My church, and the forces of Hades will not overpower it.*

As we reflect on this verse, we need to release our minds to receive some collateral revelation. The above statements are realities of the true church. Please do not judge today's church due to its painfully apparent flaws; instead, as you worship God and wait for the unfolding of His Kingdom, look for the true church to emerge. The church is in the process of becoming a pure—and mighty—bride! (See, for example, Revelation 19:7–8.)

With Jesus' historic declaration in Matthew 16:18 fixed in your mind, let us carefully proceed to talk about it in light of the verse that follows it. First, what might our initial observation or inquiry to the Lord be after hearing His words about the church? There was probably no time in between Jesus' two declarations in verses 18 and 19 to ask Him any questions. However, if there had been, we might have begun by asking, "Now, Lord, if You are going to build the church, what about my responsibilities? Is there anything I can do?" In verse 19, Jesus gives two succinct, transformational truths about the Kingdom that supply the answer:

+ *"I will give you the keys of the Kingdom of heaven...."*

+ *"...and whatever you bind on earth is already bound in heaven, and whatever you loose on earth is already loosed in heaven."*

Seven Suppositions

We can look at Matthew 16:18–19 as a defining treatise on the relationship between the church and the Kingdom of God. Jesus emphasizes two things that He will do (and is doing): (1) He will build the church, and (2) He will give keys to its constituents in relation to the Kingdom. As we examine the truths found in this passage, let me suggest the following points as valid suppositions regarding the Kingdom, the keys, and the church that will build on our discussion from the previous chapter.

1. The Kingdom is not the church, and it never will be. The church is not the Kingdom, and it never has been. They are not synonymous.

2. The Kingdom and the church are not equivalent. The Kingdom has existed from eternity, while the church came into being at Pentecost. The Kingdom is already established; the church is under construction; the Kingdom is perfect; the church is being perfected.

3. The Kingdom does not fit within the church; the church fits within the Kingdom.

4. The church must never be perceived as complete without the Kingdom, while the Kingdom is completed by the church that Jesus is building. The Kingdom will never be understood until it is acknowledged as the whole of which the church is a part; the church will never be understood until it is perceived to be connected with the Kingdom as its earthly expression. Further, a working understanding of both concepts awaits our comprehension of how one fits with the other. Our clarity regarding this is boosted by Jesus' statements, *"I will build My church,"* and *"I will give you the keys of the Kingdom."*

5. The nature of the promised keys—keys of the *Kingdom*—is significant to how Jesus will build the church. The adventure of building the church is connected to what we do with the keys He gives us.

6. Discovering and using the keys of the Kingdom is an essential aspect of our calling to *"seek first the kingdom of God"* (Matthew 6:33).

7. If we don't understand these concepts, we are destined for confusion regarding both the church and the Kingdom until we do comprehend them—and put them into effect.

What Do The "Keys" Imply?

Jesus never specifically identified the keys He promised us. This might be considered incomplete information for us, thereby creating confusion and frustration. Are we left to merely surmise what they might be? I believe it is not the absence of *specifics* concerning the meaning of the keys that is the real problem, but rather our failure to realize their *general* and *wide-ranging* meaning. If we can understand and begin to use them as they were meant to be used, this will be one of the better days of our lives!

We who have been redeemed have been granted keys vital to the operation of God's Kingdom on earth. Essentially, the keys of the Kingdom symbolize power, especially as the capacity to generate change. When we exercise the Kingdom keys, God releases His power into our circumstances on earth. In my view, the following concepts are what Jesus was referring to when He used the symbolism of keys.

Keys speak of *ownership.* Everything belongs to God, including the keys to which Jesus referred. However, He confers to us secondary ownership, giving us the privilege to use them. Such ownership grants us as key holders the right to employ the keys under divine direction. Thus, you and I own much more than we can imagine. Yet we should keep in mind that merely owning something without also having the corresponding revelation and sense of responsibility toward it is not enough.

Keys speak of *access.* Generally, when we see a locked door, we may assume that something has been intentionally placed behind that door that can be accessed only by those who have the key to its specific lock. When we find the key that fits the lock, we gain the advantage of access. We may safely conclude that God has nothing in His possession that is not accessible, under certain conditions, to His children. As the King of heaven and earth, He gives us stock in His Kingship and all His resources.

Keys speak of *inherent value*. The very existence of a key is a statement that something of value is (or has the potential to be) connected with it. To be protected and productive, many things of value require limited exposure; that is why they are often put under lock and key, to be accessed and used only by the authorized.

Keys speak of *authority.* No key has much intrinsic worth in itself; yet having a key and using it can make a world of difference to the key holder. The very position of being the bearer of a key prepares the possessor to activate the authority of ownership. For example, a business owner may give an employee a key to a strongbox, and that key, given and received, elevates the level of the employee's position of influence and potential. God is the ultimate Authority, and He gives us keys that elevate us toward our true potential as co-laborers and co-heirs with Jesus.

Keys speak of *responsibility*. When a person in authority gives a key to a subordinate, the latter stands in a position not only of influence and potential, but also of serious responsibility. And the greater the key, the greater the responsibility. However, if the subordinate is ignorant about the meaning and purpose of the key, they won't take any action with it, even though they have been given legitimate authority to do so.

If authority suggests responsibility, then ultimate authority suggests ultimate responsibility. The Giver of the keys of the Kingdom in none other than Jesus Christ, the Son of the living God. He has stated, *"All authority has been given to Me in heaven and on earth. Go, therefore, and make disciples of all nations.... And remember, I am with you always, to the end of the age"* (Matthew 28:18–20). We are responsible for operating under Jesus' ultimate authority and in His domain.

> *When Jesus gave us the keys to Kingdom living,*
> *He gave us a whole key ring,*
> *with all the keys we would ever need.*

Keys speak of *promotion*. I have found that when God is ready to grant one of His children a spiritual (or even an earthly) promotion, He generally presents them with a problem that is locked away from their normal ability to understand, and that will serve to open other spiritual mysteries in the future. He will persist until that person begins to search for the answer (key) and finally finds the one that fits the lock to their problem. I believe that when Jesus gave us the keys to Kingdom living, He gave us a whole key ring, with all the keys you and I would ever need. With the twists and turns we experience in life and in ministry, there is always a key for our particular situation, a means of entry into mystery and revelation, or an exit from difficulty and confusion that restores us to peace and freedom. The payoff is always a promotion that will give glory to God and bring good to others.

Keys speak of *confidence*. My rather long life has been marked by mysteries, curious health-related events, severe personal losses, and other conditions that I had little understanding of how to cope with. In each of these episodes, about the time I opened my mouth to ask God, "Why?" His gracious and encouraging answer went something like this: "I knew you would take the gift of wonder and pain and make something beautiful of it that is also helpful for others. Make Me proud to be your Father, and I will benefit you in the process."

This idea was affirmed to me when someone wanted to know my secret to sticking with it through thick and thin during fifty years in ministry, asking, "How have you maintained your faith and endurance through it all?" I was almost taken aback by my own answer, because it was rather sudden and surprisingly simple: "I got up the same number of times I got knocked down." After I said that, my first thought was, *Now that was a downright "earthy" answer!* But before long, a little idea trotted into my frontal lobes: *Did it ever occur to you that God is pleased not only to extend favor to you and to have faith in you but also to allow these strange happenings in order to bring good to everyone involved, including you?* Essentially, God allowed me to get knocked down in order for me to make the choice to get up again in fulfillment of His purposes.

When I think about how God gives us keys for whatever He entrusts to us, I am reminded of the following truth:

> *We know that all things work together for the good of those who love God: those who are called according to His purpose.* (Romans 8:28)

The above verse is followed immediately by a passage that explains the "Why."

> *For those He foreknew He also predestined to be **conformed to the image of His Son**, so that He would be the firstborn among many brothers. And those He predestined, He also called; and those He called, He also justified; and those He justified, He also glorified.*
> (Romans 8:29–30)

God works all things together for good by using them to conform us to the image of Jesus and to enable us to fulfill our calling in Him. Has it occurred to you that God seems to "reward" the fiercest blessings to those who trust Him and love Him most deeply? Here are some Scriptures that support this idea but are not likely to make it onto a refrigerator-door magnet:

> *Many adversities come to the one who is righteous, but the LORD delivers him from them all.* (Psalm 34:19)

> *It was good for me to be afflicted so that I could learn Your statutes.* (Psalm 119:71)

> *I know, LORD, that Your judgments are just and that You have afflicted me fairly.* (Psalm 119:75)

Is it any wonder that Teresa of Ávila is quoted as saying, in effect, "God, I am not amazed that You have as few friends as You have, from the way You treat the ones You've got!" Perhaps she said this half in pain and half in honest inquiry, but how many of us have felt the same way at times? Could it be that suffering in obedience is, in fact, a Kingdom key? We will return to this thought later.

Let us realize that the keys of the Kingdom are all around us, within reach, ready to be recognized and empowered, fitting into locks corresponding to our painful inability to understand our circumstances, and leading to liberating truths discovered behind formerly closed doors.

Standard Equipment for Kingdom Living

The above points describe what I consider to be the general symbolism of the keys of the Kingdom that Jesus has given to us. Because He invites us to discover and employ these keys, we should keep in mind that whatever the keys of the Kingdom are, they have been given to us as standard equipment for living the Kingdom life and engaging in Kingdom ministry. We should also remember that every gift our King gives us is, in effect, still owned by Him. After all, we are joints heirs with Jesus, and that is the arrangement for eternity. But everything we use for Him will be multiplied. In a related way, God asks and authorizes us to give materially to others with a radical generosity out of what He gives us; yet we never lose what we give away, because we ultimately receive it back from Him—with much more added to it. (See Luke 6:38.) Giving is not losing; giving is gaining! We are never more securely cared for than when giving bountifully is our way of life. It is the same with using the keys of the Kingdom.

Prospective List of Keys of the Kingdom

It is less important to memorize a list of available keys as it is to believe and behave as if every key is ours and is fully realized on an "as needed" basis. Jesus is not only the Key Giver but also the Key Keeper. And His Spirit, living in our spirits, is the Key Finder for every situation we face that requires a releasing or an unlocking. Is it fitting here to repeat that God hides nothing *from* us, only *for* us, for discovery. Or perhaps better yet, all that God hides that we need to find will ultimately be revealed in His best timing. *"It is the glory of God to conceal a matter and the glory of kings to investigate a matter"* (Proverbs 25:2).

Below is a list of prospective keys of the Kingdom that relate to the seven general suppositions about the keys we discussed earlier. Please keep in mind that it would probably be as impossible to name all the keys of the Kingdom available to us as it would be to name all the principles that apply to the entire universe. We become familiar with the various keys as we become acquainted with the nature of God's Kingdom. The secret is to get to know the King!

The first time I began to write out a list of keys, something seemed wrong about it. I soon discovered that my problem lay in the fact that I had written out the keys as a collection of words in one long sentence, and I didn't feel this format communicated the variety and power of the keys. I am therefore listing them individually at center page. Again, I know that this is not an exhaustive list of all the available keys, so feel free to add your own ideas.

I suggest that you prepare your mind to read the list by imagining a key in whatever shape or form you desire. I also recommend reading each word aloud and pausing long enough between the words to imbed them in your mind for later reference.

I have actually developed two lists, which I have titled "Obvious Keys" and "Hidden Keys," the former rather lengthy, the latter very brief. (Get ready for a surprise in that second list. You will know why later.) You may recognize the first fifteen or so qualities as coming from Galatians 5:22–23 and 2 Peter 1:5–7. We will discuss these particular characteristics more fully following the lists.

Obvious Keys of the Kingdom

LOVE

JOY

PEACE

PATIENCE

KINDNESS

GOODNESS

FAITHFULNESS (or FAITH)

GENTLENESS

SELF-CONTROL

FAITH (second mention)

GOODNESS (second mention)

KNOWLEDGE

SELF-CONTROL (second mention)

ENDURANCE

GODLINESS

BROTHERLY AFFECTION

LOVE (second mention)

FORGIVENESS

HONOR

WISDOM

WITNESS

FOCUS

MEMORY

IDENTITY

OPENNESS

GODLINESS

RECEPTIVITY

HONESTY

SENSITIVITY

HUMILITY

PERSEVERENCE

INSIGHTFULNESS

MERCIFULNESS

GRACIOUSNESS (as in extending grace)

RESTFULNESS

PRAYERFULNESS

PRAISEFULNESS

TRUTHFULNESS

QUIETNESS

CONFIDENCE

OBEDIENCE

SINCERITY

SECURITY

BOLDNESS

INNOCENCE

TRANSPARENCY

SIMPLICITY

ACCEPTANCE

OPTIMISM

EXPECTATION

You will notice that four qualities—love, faith, goodness, and self-control—are listed twice. This is because they are included not only in the list of the fruit of the Spirit from Galatians 5:22–23, but also in the list of spiritual characteristics from 2 Peter 1:5–7, and I wanted these individual sets of qualities to remain intact. The set from 2 Peter is listed in relation to God giving us *"everything required for life and godliness"* (2 Peter 1:3). It is worth noting that in Galatians, love is mentioned first, while in 2 Peter, love is mentioned last. It seems as if, in the Galatians passage, love is the source from which all the other qualities flow, while in the 2 Peter passage, the accumulated qualities build up to love as the ultimate quality, or key. Apparently, the first passage relates to personal *being*, while the latter relates to personal *behavior*. In the Kingdom, authentic living is not only in *being* but also in *doing* that flows out of being. We do what we do because of who we are. If we are faithful in our being, our internal integrity and belief will prompt our behavior, and our actions will reflect that belief.

> *Godly qualities are also keys or principles that
> can generate power to effect change.*

I would not be surprised if you are just a bit disappointed with the above list of obvious keys, not because you consider these qualities to have no value, but because you were hoping I might reveal some "new" information on the keys of the Kingdom. Actually, each item is of great value as a character trait or attribute, something we would wish to exhibit in our lives all the time. However, these qualities that we so earnestly desire to be expressed in our lives are also keys or principles that, when applied, generate power to effect change, opening doors to a new level of living. Again, there are keys all around us, all the time, that will "fit" any and all situations. The keys are employed and activated by our prayers as we intercede for these circumstances.

With this perspective in mind, look back over the list and declare, with thanksgiving, that each of these qualities is yours in Christ and will surely be a "key" to opening and closing, binding and releasing, in regard to various situations in your life. I have found that thinking this way about these admirable qualities has exploded the concept of the keys of the Kingdom in my mind. I will never be the same because of this discovery.

Hidden Keys of the Kingdom

Let us now turn to the second list, entitled "Hidden Keys of the Kingdom." I have no desire to rain on your picnic, but there are certain experiences I want to mention that most of us would never consider keys to anything useful; nevertheless, they are powerful keys:

DISAPPOINTMENT

WAITING

WEAKNESS

SUFFERING

Let's explore why these often unwelcome experiences are Kingdom keys.

Disappointment

Disappointment is a common human experience that begins early in life and is continually repeated (sometimes, it seems to multiply) from childhood until death. The very word rings in our ears with ominous tones. Every disappointment is...well, disappointing. Moreover, if a person does not acknowledge and deal with unresolved disappointment, it can be repeated in every successive generation, touching them and their descendants spirit, soul, and body, so that life amounts to one huge disorder.

But could disappointment, properly assessed, processed, and addressed, be a strategic key in Kingdom affairs? What if this many-headed monster could become a mere memory, cleansed of its terror and attendant miseries, and transformed into one of the *"all things"* Paul mentioned in Romans 8:28 as working together for our good and God's glory?

Let me tell you again that, honestly, my life has been a catalog of griefs and disappointments. I have previously mentioned some of these, including the deaths of two beloved spouses. Years earlier, my first son died when he was barely old enough to have a name, and I brought my wife home to an empty room and an empty cradle with an empty heart. I have also experienced heart attacks, surgeries, betrayals, and the deaths of spiritual sons.... But, wait—if the prefix *dis-* in *disappointment* signifies, as in its original meaning, the "undoing of an appointment," every such disappointment leads to a new *re*-appointment in Kingdom life. Every disappointment is transformed into something new: God's appointment!

If you think I was complaining or seeking pity when I mentioned my sorrows and disappointments above, let me put your mind to rest. As I expressed earlier, every time I revisit those memories, my heart is now filled with thanksgiving and praise. By the grace of God, my faith in His eternal and infinite goodness remains unshaken. As I said, every time I got knocked down, I got up again—not to limp through life with self-pity and disappointment weighing me down, but to move forward with more joy than ever before, and with even more excitement about the absolute satisfaction of living the Kingdom life.

Somehow, in each of those experiences, with trembling frame and flowing tears, I chose to praise God for His providence, and He shaped every disappointment into a memory stone of that perfect providence. Now I know that disappointment can truly be a key in Kingdom affairs. The secret to this key, as with all the others, is to always turn toward the Kingdom and its King, who will transform what may seem to be disorder and disaster into His glory, for our greater good!

Waiting

Have you ever heard anyone say, "I just can't wait until the next time I get to wait?" On a scale of one to ten (ten being the worst), most of us would rank the experience of waiting as an eleven! But again, what if waiting is a key that is just *waiting* to fit into the situation that has precipitated this unwelcome delay in your life? Try applying the Kingdom key of waiting. You will be surprised at its benefits, I guarantee it. If you connect your waiting to the King and His Kingdom, a redefinition of the nature and purpose of waiting will begin in your heart and mind. You can link your waiting to some specific Scriptures, such as the following:

They that wait upon the LORD shall renew their strength; they shalt mount up with wings as eagles; they shall run, and not be weary; and they shall walk, and not faint. (Isaiah 40:31 KJV)

The LORD is a God of justice. Blessed are all who wait for Him! (Isaiah 30:18 NIV)

God…acts on behalf of those who wait for Him. (Isaiah 64:4 NIV)

Now, imagine yourself as a server in a restaurant. Pick up your serving towel, drape it gently over your left forearm, and softly say, "Father, may I wait on You?" Your waiting will honor and please Him, and He will meet your need.

Weakness

Another surprising Kingdom key is weakness. We have all felt weak, but have we ever investigated the reason for this feeling? Could it be because we *are* weak? Tune in to an imagined conversation between the apostle Paul and the Lord, based on 2 Corinthians 12:1–10.

"Lord, I am pleading with You. I'm in pain, and I need some relief!"

(Silence.)

"Lord, I am in great pain, would You please do something?"

(More silence.)

"Lord, it's getting unbearable; could You, You know, kind of, H-E-L-P?"

Note: This conversation may have been repeated many times with increasing urgency on Paul's part.

Finally, God speaks: "Paul, My grace is all you need, for My power is perfected in your weakness."

Paul answers, "Well, if that's the case, I will brag up a storm about my weaknesses so that Christ's power may dwell upon me. While I am at it, I will be pleased with '*insults, catastrophes, persecutions, and…pressures, because of Christ. For when I am weak, then I am strong.*'"

Paul turned the seeming tragedy of his weakness into the triumph of God's strength. The weakness of his pain, coupled with faith, became a key of the Kingdom!

Suffering

Here is another verse you will probably never find on a refrigerator magnet: "*In the world you will have tribulation*" (John 16:33 NKJV)! As we live in this world, we all undergo various types of difficulty, suffering, and trial. However, let's remember the remainder of the verse: "*But be of good cheer, I [Jesus] have overcome the world*" (NKJV).

One more bit of encouragement from Jesus for those who suffer for His sake:

> *You are blessed when they insult and persecute you and falsely say every kind of evil against you because of Me. Be glad and rejoice, because your reward is great in heaven. For that is how they persecuted the prophets who were before you.* (Matthew 5:11–12)

I rest my case. Suffering is a vital key in the realm of God's rule!

The Key to Everything

Permit me to conclude by repeating the following for emphasis: *all* the keys of the Kingdom have been given to us. We will never, ever, face a situation, a closed door, a dilemma, a seemingly option-less quandary, or impossible odds for which, within the realm of the Kingdom, there is not an appropriate key! We do not have to worry about it because it is already ours by divine decree. We are to ask, seek, and knock until the key manifests. And then we are to "keep on keeping on" asking, seeking, and knocking for additional keys in other situations. (See Matthew 7:7–8.)

I know that someone reading these words is stuck in the slough of despondency, or has the piercing sword of distressing conditions hanging over their head, or is caught up in a cyclone of events that are out of their control, with the future anything but inviting. *Impossible* could easily be the word that best describes the fix in which you find yourself. What should you do?

KEY ALERT! Go directly to God, who is the Key Keeper, the Key Giver, and the Key Finder, and you will happily discover that He—Father, Son, and Holy Spirit—is the Key to everything, and the ultimate Key that fits all! Only God can truly bring resolution to your situation, and the key to this resolution is ready and waiting to be used. Stay before Him until the answer you seek becomes evident.

Now you have the secret to the keys of the Kingdom: Jesus is building His church. The church is His possession and cannot fail. He has given believers Kingdom keys for the exercise of divine authority in binding what heaven has bound and in loosing what heaven has loosed. These keys are the governing principles that we need in order to promote the affairs of the Kingdom of God on earth. They are Spirit-given and Spirit-governed in the hands of the Spirit-filled. Look to the keys, apply them to your life, and begin to use them to bind and release!

8

KINGDOM WARFARE

"Wherever there is a church obeying the words and doing the works of Jesus there is an outpost of the Kingdom of God. And the outpost is always in the middle of enemy territory. Count on it! Any turf you win you have to defend. The forces of evil may fall back, but they won't permanently retreat."
—*John Wimber*[12]

"If we could but show the world that being committed to Christ is no tame, humdrum, sheltered monotony but indeed the greatest adventure the human spirit could ever know, the world, standing outside, would come in to pay allegiance to the Christ, and we could expect the greatest revival since Pentecost!"
—*Bill Bright*[13]

---

12. John Wimber, *The Way In Is the Way On* (Boise, ID: Ampelon Publishing, 2006), 146–147.
13. Bill Bright, spoken at the American Baptist Encampment, Oshkosh, WI, 1957.

Kingdoms in Conflict

No emphasis or message will more immediately draw the attention of the enemy than that of the Kingdom of God. Satan, with his kingdom of darkness, hates God and His Kingdom of light. What we call *spiritual warfare* is the manifestation of these kingdoms in conflict. Jesus thoughtfully informed us,

> *From the days of John the Baptist until now, the Kingdom of heaven has been suffering violence, and the violent have been seizing it by force.* (Matthew 11:12)

In his kingdom of darkness, the devil is the self-acclaimed anti-King. Everything that Jesus is for, Satan, in both disposition and activity, is against. He is antichrist, antilife, anti-truth, and anti-God. (Thus, in a negative sense, he is the best detector of what is right, noble, holy, and good.) This is why, when we begin to preach and practice the truth about any area of Kingdom reality, the devil cannot help but automatically contest it. Anything that reminds him of his lamentable past, his futile present, and his doomed future invokes his immediate protest and wrath.

> When we preach and practice the truth of the Kingdom,
> the devil automatically contests it.

It will help you to understand—and respond to—many events and experiences if you will determine to remember what you have just read. Whenever you say or do something related to the eternal Kingdom of God, it will greatly disturb your enemy and his demons (and often, by the way, his human supporters). If you had been in numerous battles and lost as many times as Satan has, you would not be surprised by his wrathful reactions.

Welcome to Kingdom warfare! The fact that we bear the name of Jesus precipitates the waging of battles between the forces of good and evil in and around our lives. We live in an antagonistic world of fiery fighting fueled by the devil and his evil spirits, a reality that much of the world either passively or actively denies. The fact is, it would be difficult to overstate the certainty of the existence of the kingdom of darkness. It would be frightening to all of us if we were given a look into the reality of the diabolical and malevolent forces of evil in the very atmosphere through which we navigate our lives every day.

Rising Above Complacency and a Deficient Message

The following may be a shocking statement, but I am going to make it anyway: if you are not personally experiencing some level of spiritual warfare in your life, I suggest that you immediately check your decision for Jesus and your relationship to Him. It might be that the devil has you just where he wants you—comfortable, complacent, and quite satisfied to make it to heaven with as little effort as possible.

It is my deep conviction that such a mind-set is connected to one of the greatest problems with Christianity at present. The purpose of much preaching and evangelism today is to try to convince people to have a personal relationship with Jesus, but with a primary emphasis on their going to heaven. There is pressure on pastors and churches to get the maximum number of people "saved." This is why there is inevitably a problem with people's motivation to follow through the implications of their newfound faith, and with leaders' incentive to emphasize post-conversion discipleship and an awareness of Kingdom realities, such as spiritual warfare.

There is nothing wrong with evangelistic preaching if it leads to effective living. Godly behavior and empowered ministry should directly follow our decision to trust Jesus as Savior and to follow Him as Lord. As it says in Matthew 6:33, "Seek first the Kingdom of God *and His righteousness*." While bringing people to salvation through Jesus is a noble goal, it should not be carried on to the neglect of *"training in righteousness"* (2 Timothy 3:16), among both brand-new converts and current believers.

My own Christian experience illustrates this point. I was saved at ten years of age by being led to ask Jesus into my heart. I know now that the gospel being preached to my age group was deficient, centering on a single experience of conversion. Again, it isn't that this message was wrong, but it was tragically incomplete in its neglect or absence of further teachings on the believers' quality of life following the crisis decision of accepting Jesus as Savior. Similar to what I described above, we saw the world as one ripened harvest field ready for the ingathering of souls. I was incited to passion and concern for lost sinners through a strong, emotional plea to "rescue the perishing and care for the dying," and it was a success as far as it went. When I was twenty years of age and preparing for the ministry, the denomination-wide goal for the year was "a million more in fifty-four and every Baptist a tither."

I almost weep when I remember this era of my life. I had been saved more than ten years earlier, had finished college, and was about to begin pastoring my first church. I remember wanting to be known as a powerful preacher, hot after souls and building a huge church. My first pastorate was a small congregation at the bend of the road between two small, south-central Texas towns in the open country. I sought after what I was taught in college and seminary, wanting to see people converted, baptized, and then good church members and tithers. That is about all I asked for, and there wasn't much room for anything else.

In my religious smugness, I experienced no spiritual warfare (that I knew of). At that time, I had little understanding of the Kingdom—and the devil has no fear of a Kingdom-less church or a Kingdom-less Christian. However, in His grace, God related to me and my ministry at the level of my spiritual awareness. As I mentioned earlier, I respected the Holy Spirit as part of the Trinity but held Him at a safe distance. Blessings and numbers of converts were sufficient to make me think I was a success—that is, by the criteria we held sacred, namely, the statistics by which we had learned to measure our success. With some pastors, it was a joking matter as we spoke about the "holy trinity" of buildings, budgets, and baptisms.

Thus, I was deceived by systemic success. Little did I know that my deception about spiritual realities allowed the devil to gain victories in my life without my even putting up a fight. Deception is, well, deceiving. It's like sleep—you usually don't realize you're asleep until you wake up.

However, the power of Kingdom truth will expose such deception. Consequently, it will also stir up a new level of spiritual activity in the realms of darkness against us. This is what happened to me as I began to understand more about the Kingdom message. It was around this time that I had a new interest in, and exercise of, spiritual warfare. Of all things, our church was thrust into the ministry of dealing with demons. And, I might add, with a great deal of success attending that ministry. Yet at the time, I didn't know enough to move on to Kingdom living, loving, and ministry.

Notice that the title of this chapter is called "Kingdom Warfare," which I define as spiritual warfare carried to the point of ultimate intensity. The rediscovery of the Kingdom message will always stir up a level of conflict not experienced in the normal, human level of church activity. It must be recognized and remembered that there was no deliverance activity in Jesus' ministry until the moment He was recognized as the Messiah and Son of God. From the time of His affirmation by the Father at His baptism and the revelation of His essential identity, the devil and his demons flanked His ministry wherever He went. (See, for example, Matthew 3:13–4:11.)

Moreover, recall that one of the first indications of the Kingdom's arrival that Jesus cited was this: *"If I drive out demons by the Spirit of God, then the Kingdom of God has come to you"* (Matthew 12:28). At least a third of the ministry of Jesus was a catalog of conflict between Him and the powers of darkness. He never met a demon He could not cast out, defeat, or set to flight after addressing. Similarly, today, our encounters with the demonic are clear proof that the Kingdom has come and is in our midst.

The War Is Already Won

When we enter the Kingdom life, we receive all the resources that were available to Jesus in His ministry on earth. The reason Kingdom truth is so effective in warfare is that a proper Kingdom view of everything forms a grid for our growing faith, daring prayer, and lasting joy. When the

Kingdom provides a basis for all our thinking, the enemy will experience continual frustration in his attempts to thrust his agenda of lies on us.

Thus, as the Kingdom message and mentality are restored to the curriculum of the church, the rising tide of spiritual perception and Kingdom activity among believers will prove more than the devil can deal with. I cannot imagine what changes will occur as we return to seeking the Kingdom of God first and above all! Spiritual warfare will be characterized by joyous successes and victories; casting out demons will even become a happy ministry, not a heavy one; and signs and wonders of all sorts, including deliverance, will be dispersed in the trail of our ministries.

Some believers are afraid of Satan and his attacks against God's Kingdom—and against them personally. But this is the time for standing, not for ducking and running from the conflict! Hold your ground. Be strong. Don't let up, don't back up, and don't give up. You are a victor. You are a citizen of the Kingdom of God, with Kingdom rights within you, Kingdom resources behind you, Kingdom friends beside you, and Kingdom authority and personnel directing you (the Father, the Son, and the Holy Spirit, with their messenger angels and protective angels).

> *We are fighting from victory, not toward it. The enemy's defeat was already accomplished on the cross.*

Dress yourself daily in the wardrobe found in your Kingdom manual, the Bible. (See, for example, Ephesians 6:10–18.) It is replete with sufficient information within its covers to equip you for victory in your inner life and success in your outer life. The phrase "defeated Christian" is really an oxymoron. You can be a Christian, or you can be defeated, but if you can put those two descriptions together to describe one life, we need to talk!

It must have been more than seventy years ago that I heard an old preacher say something like this: "There is no such thing as a losing fight against the devil on the part of a Christian!" I wanted to argue with that sweeping statement. Wasn't I a Christian? Most certainly! Had I been defeated? Yes, frequently and continuously. I was living proof of my doubt about victory being certain in spiritual warfare. Today, I see things differently, and I believe that the old preacher was right. As long as we continue the fight, there is victory. We lose only when we *stop* fighting.

Remember, you are fighting from victory, not toward it. The battle was won on your behalf by Christ before you reported for action. The defeat of the devil has already been accomplished on the cross. That means the spoils of war belong to you! Receive them. Don't wait until the enemy attacks again—beat him to it. Confess your essential identity as a child of the living God, your riches in authority and power, and your standing in the courts of heaven.

Victory Is Not for the Solitary

I have found that many Christians are living in abject defeat with regard to spiritual warfare because of their lack of interaction with other believers. It is absolutely necessary for you, dear believer, to have regular communication and contact with others who share your faith and love for God. Living, vital relationships are indispensable for Christians, both in their personal lives and their community life together. The enemy has a weapon that causes defeat everywhere he uses it—it is called *isolation*. Isolation promotes weakness and division, which allows the devil to singularly defeat believers.

The church is described as a body, all connected to the Head, who is Christ. We were designed for interaction. We need each other, and we should never have to carry on spiritual warfare alone. The prophet Malachi registered the Lord's response to the interaction of God's people in his day:

> At that time those who feared the LORD spoke to one another. The LORD took notice and listened. So a book of remembrance was written before Him for those who feared Yahweh and had regard for His name.   (Malachi 3:16)

Imagine that! God Himself takes notice of our conversations with other believers and records them in a book of remembrance. He wants us to agree together to spread His love, His will, and His purposes on earth. A high level of interaction in the body of Christ should be inevitable, ever-growing, and a source of power and widespread influence. True believers should be working together and communicating at every level and in every venue of life.

Nothing would please me more than for you to become more and more interactive with other believers because of this book. Don't try to wage spiritual warfare alone! Pray that God would begin to connect you with like-minded believers who are learning the true nature of His Kingdom and who understand the need to fight back against the powers of darkness.

A New Day in Kingdom Warfare

The experience of writing this book has been like none other, because it has occasioned the bringing together of almost twenty years of my thoughts on the subject of the Kingdom, as well as a review of my earlier published works. In the process, I have been arrested by several chapters in my book *Much More*, which was written in the continuing heat, fading as it was, of the tremendous awakening at my church. Let me quote from chapter 10, entitled "The Much More of Spiritual Warfare: Wake Up to Another World." I have recently become convinced that I was saying "much more" then than I knew. I was talking about a level of warfare that was not extant at the time and wouldn't exist until the Kingdom message began to be recovered. In fact, I believe I was writing about the level of Kingdom warfare that is being fought today.

At that time, there was little sense of the reality of the devil, demons, angels, and the intensity of the spiritual struggle around them. The following words are more applicable today than at that time because there is currently an open assault on the Christian faith, message, and practice. The work of Satan in the world has never been more painfully obvious. It seems that we daily receive reports worldwide of the enemy's attack on everything we consider of value—his intentions calculated to destroy the church and every trace of God in the world. Meanwhile, on the home front, we are calling sin and rebellion acceptable, and even perversion tolerable and law-ful. Morals are in a freefall, rebellion is rampant, atheism and skepticism are shouting loudly against our cherished beliefs, and political correctness tries to make what we believe look foolish; and indeed, to the world it is foolish! The church seems to have lost its voice and its way. Sad to say, it has apparently also lost its courage.

Doesn't this quote from *Much More* sound more like today than the 1970s?

> But alas, there are many Christians who are not even aware that there is a war on. I am convinced that this group comprises the greater part of those whose names are listed (on church rolls) among the saints. Then there are those who suspicion that there is a war on but can't seem to decide whose side they are on. They would like to get by without committing themselves because they are trying to make the best of both worlds. Then there are those who have discovered that there is a war on, know whose side they are on, but don't seem to be sure as to the outcome. They are dis-couraged, dejected, and defeated. Then, bless the Lord, there are those who have discovered that there is a war on, know whose side they are on, and are certain of the outcome because Christ has already finished the victory. These are they who do not faint in the battle because they have learned the secret—VICTORY IS OURS!

> No sooner did the Holy Spirit come upon Jesus than the Holy Spirit led Him into the wilderness for His encounter with Satan. This encounter was to be an example of every other encounter they were to have…. My Savior beat him and beat him badly. He has given us the use of His name that we might bring to bear upon the earth the power of that victory over the devil.

> I am discovering a very interesting fact, in that the opening of the eyes of the average Christian to the world of the supernatural, the spiritual struggle, and the existence of the devil and demons

brings an immediate explosion of joy and delight in his relationship with Christ.[14]

Amazing, isn't it, that the statement you just read was first written over four decades ago? Additionally, my words from the back cover of *Much More* kindled in me a new excitement about the days in which we now live:

> I have a greater sense than I have ever had that God is up to something. There is a strange moving in the land! There is a fresh stirring in the tops of the mulberries! There are harbingers of holy things to come all around us! I am under the awesome impression that we are on the verge of the greatest Spirit-visitation since the beginning of Christendom.[15]

Could the escalation of division, hate, and violence in the world—and the resulting depression, discouragement, and distress among people—be the trumpet heralding a new day in Kingdom warfare? I say, "Yes!"

As I wrote earlier, we need to back away from the bad news that we read in the newspapers or on the Internet, or that we watch on television (it would perhaps be better called the "olds" than the "news"), with its "paralysis of analysis." We are in the vortex of a warfare that many people have overlooked in their observations of the problems of the world around us. Collectively, we are wringing our hands and furrowing our brows in worry as if there were nothing we could do about it. I beg to differ with that disposition!

> *Kingdom-seeking will lead to Kingdom-finding,*
> *Kingdom-living, and Kingdom-loving.*

---

14. Jack R. Taylor, *Much More* (Bedford, Texas, Burkhart Books, 2013), 102. Original published by Broadman, 1972, 116–117.
15. Ibid, back cover.

Behind the forbidding scenes of Kingdom warfare, we may behold the smiling face of God, calling us to enter the greatest season ever known on the face of the earth. If you are going to fight a war, this is the one to choose. It is unlike the usual, physical warfare, which anticipates the dreaded loss of personnel necessary for victory, while, at the same time, fearfully considers the possibility of defeat. Not so in this war! Remember that the war to which the Kingdom beckons us has already been won. The victory is eternally secure in Christ and has been credited to us. All we have to do is manage the supremacy, authority, and power that our King has given us. *We must not fail to address this war.*

Over the past several decades, there has been a surge of information on spiritual warfare, accompanied by a powerful anointing for deliverance ministry, which, in turn, has generated many effective spiritual warriors. The ministry of deliverance has been seen by many as a viable application of the gospel of grace. Many bold souls have entered the fray with confidence and eagerness. But the church in general has frowned upon the "weird stuff" surrounding the ministry of separating people—even believers—from demons that were afflicting them. In the culture-bound church, it just didn't seem sufficiently dignified to be a justifiable practice. I still get calls from various areas across this great land asking if I know of anybody in that general vicinity who knows how to deal with demons. Sadly, in most cases, I have to answer in the negative.

This is about to change! Kingdom-seeking will lead to Kingdom-finding, and Kingdom-finding will lead to Kingdom-living, and Kingdom-living will lead to Kingdom-loving. These developments will arouse, expose, and terrorize the hosts of hell. Kingdom warriors will rise with Kingdom faith, and Kingdom faith will seize Kingdom victory.

As Martin Luther observed:

And though this world, with devils filled,
Should threaten to undo us,
We will not fear, for God hath willed
His truth to triumph through us:
The Prince of Darkness grim,
We tremble not for him;

His rage we can endure,
For lo, his doom is sure;
One little word shall fell him.

That word above all earthly powers,
No thanks to them, abideth;
The Spirit and the gifts are ours
Through him who with us sideth:
Let goods and kindred go,
This mortal life also;
The body they may kill:
God's truth abideth still;
His Kingdom is forever.[16]

Welcome to the battlefront. The King has your back, and you're covered by the Kingdom!

---

16. Martin Luther, "A Mighty Fortress Is Our God," 1529, *Hymns for the Living Church* (Carol Stream, IL: Hope Publishing Company, 1974), 11. Emphasis added.

PART 3

SEEKING FIRST THE KINGDOM

9

SEEK FIRST THE KINGDOM: LIFE'S MOST IMPORTANT ADVENTURE

Seek first the Kingdom of God and His righteousness, and all these things will be provided for you. (Matthew 6:33)

Every serious believer must be committed to searching for God's highest and best...His Kingdom. Jesus' command in Matthew 6:33 is, first of all, indicative of the fact that the Kingdom is available to seek and to manifest on earth. Second, the command *"seek"* is given as a "durative verb," which indicates the aspect of continuation.[17] In other words, we are not to seek the Kingdom at intervals but consistently, repeatedly, constantly. Third, the word *"first"* denotes that we are to seek the Kingdom as our top priority. We are not to seek just part of the Kingdom part of the time, but all of the Kingdom all of the time. Fourth, we are to include *"righteousness"* in our Kingdom search, which means that in seeking the Kingdom, we will find its inevitable expression in righteous, holy living.

When Jesus made this statement about seeking first the Kingdom, He had just been talking about those who were preoccupied with the pursuit of wealth, food, and clothing. He has nothing against our seeking to fulfill

17. Charles F. Pfeiffer and Everett F. Harrison, eds. *The Wycliffe Bible Commentary* (Chicago: Moody Press, 1962), 940.

basic human needs, which is a natural desire. Rather, He targeted our sin of worry in the light of our relationship with God as our loving Father who promises to provide for us. We are to heed one command about worry: "Don't!" Jesus said, in essence, "Don't worry about what to eat, what to wear, and where to live. Look at the birds of the sky: they don't sow or reap, yet your heavenly Father feeds them. Look at the beauty of the flowers, and realize that Solomon in all his glory could not adorn himself as magnificently as God clothes them. Likewise, your Father knows everything you need, all the time, and has committed Himself to your total care." (See Matthew 6:25–32.) The great problem with worry is its emphasis on temporal things and its accompanying expectation of finding ultimate fulfillment in something apart from the Kingdom.

What Do You Seek First?

What we seek first will determine what our lives will be like. Everybody is seeking something, whether it is love, riches, renown, or another aspiration. They may find it, and they may not. People sometimes think it's better to continue searching for something, even if they never find it, than to end their search altogether in total disappointment. They reason that as long as they are seeking, they have hope that they might still find it. But if their search is outside the Kingdom of God, even if they find what they are looking for, their satisfaction will be both temporary and illusory, and their life will still be incomplete. Ultimately, whatever they were searching for will leave them sadly disappointed. Accordingly, when we seek things that people in the world have tried and found fraudulent, we can hope for no other results in our own personal searches.

We inexorably prove the uselessness of our pursuits when we refuse to seek God or put a premium on His Word. Try as we might, we cannot prove ourselves right. Looking for importance in this world, we become poster children for what happens when we seek first anything other than God. We sentence ourselves to perpetual futility, constant frustration, and endless striving. Chaos, violence, depression, hopelessness, despair, and destruction are the markers of our age and any age in which humanity does not seek God. Moreover, such foolish seeking will move us down the road toward full-blown idolatry. Richard Foster wrote,

> We are to discipline ourselves to "seek *first* the Kingdom of God." This focus must take precedence over absolutely everything. We must never allow anything, whether deed or desire, to have that place of central importance. The redistribution of the world's wealth cannot be central,…the desire for simplicity itself cannot be central. The moment any of these becomes the focus of our concern, it has become idolatry. Only one thing is to be central: the Kingdom of God. And, in fact, when the Kingdom of God is genuinely placed first, the equitable distribution of wealth, ecological concerns, the poor, simplicity, and all things necessary will be given their proper attention.[18]

God takes very personally our failure to put His Kingdom first on our search list. However, His greatest sorrow is not in His loss but in our not being wise and discerning in the business of receiving and giving the riches of His Kingdom.

An Out-of-This-World Offer

Jesus presents us with an alternative to such frustrating and empty searches that, if truly understood, only a fool would turn down. His proposition begins with a command and ends with the promise of a remarkable result. This arrangement of which He speaks is with Someone who loves us unconditionally, has the key to ultimate fulfillment in life, desires our highest good, and has unending resources that He wants to make available to us. He offers to take complete care of all our needs, both the basic kind and the advanced variety.

Doubtless, it is more fun to be independently wealthy, with enough money to be free of concerns about whether we can afford groceries next week, whether we will have enough money for next month's rent or mortgage payment, or whether we will have the funds for college tuition or a

---

18. Richard Foster, *Freedom of Simplicity* (New York: HarperOne, 2005), 104–105. Reprint edition, originally published in 1981 by Harper and Row. Emphasis is in the original.

nice vacation. Yet few people, if any, seem to have found true satisfaction in an abundance of riches.

The One requesting such a relationship is, of course, God the Father, who has spoken His invitation through His Son Jesus Christ. The Father is rich beyond imagination and has no reason to need us; but because of His great love and plans for us, He wants to count us "in" on the whole set of His eternal intentions. The King seeks us out because of the fabulous Kingdom purposes He has for the whole human family. Yet we must have the courage to qualify for such an arrangement. If we don't meet the qualification…no deal. How do we qualify? It's simple: we must belong to the Father through faith in His Son.

worthy

> *Jesus never said "Seek first…" about any other*
> *pursuit or purpose than the Kingdom.*

Let's rephrase Jesus' sweeping suggestion, for clarity and emphasis: "You look after My Kingdom, and I will look after yours. When you seek My Kingdom, you are seeking Me—your Creator and Sustainer, as well as your ultimate Resource." For those who already know Jesus—who know something of what He is like and why He wants us to seek His rule—this offer should be a no-brainer. He is One who can fully back up His proposal. Yet how hesitant most of us are to take the big leap of trust and seek Him *first*. For many people, the offer sounds too good to be true. Yet this is the promise of the Son of the living God, and it stands forever.

As I wrote at the beginning of this book, Jesus never said *"Seek first…"* about any other pursuit or purpose than the Kingdom. If we accept this proposal from Him, it grants us active participation in God's eternal enterprise. Receiving His offer might just be the best decision of your life (an extreme understatement)!

To seek God is to seek all of Him—His rule, His lifestyle, and His pleasure. Seeking the Kingdom of God and His righteousness before everything else is the key that unlocks all the benefits available in heaven and on earth. When the Kingdom is our priority, everything is ours. We have the backing of the entire universe, with all that God is and all that God has.

As I emphasized earlier, seeking the Kingdom is inevitably a dual search—for God's Kingdom and for His righteousness—with a sure promise, which is the provision of our daily needs and anything else required for fulfilling His will. To consider seeking God's Kingdom and righteousness at a time when all other searches prove to be exercises in futility is noble indeed. If desperation, hopelessness, and boredom flank us on every side, perhaps, just perhaps, it's time to change the object of our search. The kingdoms before which we have bowed have failed to produce even our basic expectations; and the fact is, most of them have blown up in our faces.

Steps to Seeking and Finding the Kingdom

Every now and then, where appropriate, I enjoy using alliteration in my teaching. There are advantages to explaining spiritual truths using words that begin with the same letter or have similar sounds or rhymes. It can be fun to do this, but it also can be easy to overdo it, sacrificing exactness in thought for similarity in sound or spelling. However, I think using alliteration in this section will enable us to understand and remember these principal steps to seeking and finding the Kingdom. Some of the steps will overlap, and they all reinforce one another.

+ Kingdom *Sightings* (experiencing the Kingdom)
+ Kingdom *Seeing* (discerning the Kingdom)
+ Kingdom *Seeking* (pursuing the Kingdom)
+ Kingdom *Seizing* and *Being Seized* by the Kingdom (taking hold of that which Christ Jesus has taken hold of us)
+ Kingdom *Speaking* (articulation of the basics of the Kingdom) and Kingdom *Sounding* (proclaiming the Kingdom)

The above steps lead to Kingdom *searching*—seeking even more of the Kingdom—and Kingdom *soaring*, in which we are raised into the atmosphere of the Kingdom, allowing it to fill our lives. Let's now explore the main steps to seeking and finding the Kingdom.

Kingdom Sightings

The first step is to become more aware of expressions and demonstrations of the Kingdom around us—what I call "Kingdom sightings." A Kingdom sighting can manifest in a variety of ways. It might be an event or visible happening for which there is no possible earthly explanation and can be attributed only to God's direct intervention. It might take the form of a particular communication from God—perhaps through Scripture, a dream, a word from someone else heard amid casual conversation that you recognize has spiritual significance, or a nugget of truth entertained for a few seconds that suddenly explodes into a chain of thoughts that reveal significant spiritual insights. It might also come as an inner transformation of our emotions or thought patterns that can only be explained as a heavenly "invasion" of healing, knowledge, or wisdom.

> *When we learn why and where to look,*
> *we will suddenly see the Kingdom sightings*
> *God is sending our way.*

Believers should regularly experience Kingdom sightings. Many of us don't think we have experienced any, but such sightings have actually been manifesting continually, as far as eternal reality is concerned. We have just not trained our spiritual eyes to see them or our spiritual ears to hear them. As we begin to understand and experience the Kingdom, such sightings will seem to occur more frequently.

Often, when I don't recognize Kingdom sightings, it is because the openness of the "child within me" has given way to my seeing as an adult, and I miss the moment. At such times, I remember this adage, sometimes painfully: "Adults are sometimes just obsolete children." Ouch! But Jesus said, "*I assure you: whoever does not welcome the Kingdom of God like a little child will never enter it*" (Luke 18:17). Let's face it—becoming an adult is accompanied by great risks that can become handicaps in life. The seldom-prayed prayer "Lord, make me like a child again" may prove life-transforming. (I will share more on this idea in a later section.)

One wise observer explained, concerning Kingdom sightings, "We don't have a seeing problem, we have a looking problem." During my eight years of theological training, nobody told me where to look or what to look for in this regard. Many of us are looking in all the wrong places because we have not known where to search. Others have been too busy or distracted to look at all. If we are merely looking at things in general, we will likely see nothing in particular. However, when we learn why and where to look, we will suddenly see Kingdom sightings that God is sending our way.

Kingdom sightings work together with Kingdom *seeing* and Kingdom *seeking* (concepts we'll cover more fully soon). Kingdom sightings can lead us to a better understanding of spiritual truth if we are able to discern God's purposes in them. For example, when Paul and Silas were imprisoned for their faith in Philippi, and were praising God at midnight in their cell, a heavenly earthquake came and shook loose their chains, prompting their jailor to recognize that God was truly with them, and causing him to ask, "*What must I do to be saved?*" (Acts 16:30). Kingdom sightings (the extraordinary witness of Paul and Silas and God's dramatic intervention on their behalf) led to Kingdom seeing (the jailor saw his spiritual need), as well as Kingdom seeking (the jailor earnestly inquired how he could enter the kingdom). Although Kingdom sightings often lead to Kingdom seeing, sometimes the reverse is true: Kingdom seeing can lead to Kingdom sightings, because as we discern and apply spiritual truth, we will experience Kingdom manifestations.

Here is a personal example of a Kingdom sighting. One time, my wife and I were traveling by plane from one state to another for multiple ministry engagements, with our destination Albuquerque, New Mexico. The time we had spent so far on the journey had been above and beyond all our expectations in terms of spiritual blessings and the powerful presence of God, and we eagerly and happily anticipated a pleasant trip. So pronounced were the joys of the recent past blessings and the prospects of future and greater blessings that I found myself singing the words to a song from a classic stage musical, with my own variation:

> Oh, what a beautiful morning,
> Oh, what a beautiful day!
> I've got a beautiful feeling
> Everything's going [His] way![19]

We soon arrived at our destination with no complications, even though we'd had to make some close connections. It seemed like a perfect day in the making! After an early arrival in beautiful Albuquerque, we received a text from Pastor Alan Hawkins that he and his wife, Gail, our spiritual son and daughter, would immediately pick us up at curbside. My "beautiful feeling about a beautiful day" continued. Then, it was only a brief ride from the airport to their lovely home where we would be staying, which was located in the foothills of rock-studded mountains towering above the landscape of the city. Everything was going His way!

But after we arrived at their house, I was suddenly struck with panic. All our checked baggage was accounted for, and Friede's carry-ons were present, but my computer bag was somehow missing. I quickly reviewed what had transpired upon our arrival at the airport and during our subsequent car ride. That settled the mystery but increased my panic. In the excitement of exchanging hugs with our hosts and loading luggage into their car, I had left my beloved computer at curbside—with all my written notes for the book you are now reading, along with literally thousands of pages of other notes, plus pictures, music, and more.

I was no longer singing. Countless thoughts assaulted my mind as we began our trip back across town to the airport: Had the bag been snatched up by someone? Had it been picked up by the airport police? Was it still sitting at curbside?

---

19. Lyrics by Oscar Hammerstein II, "Oh, What a Beautiful Morning," 1943, from *Oklahoma!*

Then Pastor Alan mentioned that a new spiritual son of his was arriving at the airport at that very moment. He called him immediately and reported our emergency, catching him just as he was checking out his rental car. This spiritual son was given the assignment of inquiring about my computer bag with the airport authorities and then calling us right back.

I anxiously breathed a quick prayer and was suddenly reminded of words I had recently written about Kingdom sightings. Then we received a phone call saying that my computer had been found by airport personnel, searched for possible explosives or drugs, and set aside just as our "angel on assignment" walked up to the lost baggage area. He asked to be given the computer bag, pleading with the authorities to hand it over to him, a perfect stranger, which was against their policy. He stated that he was acting on the emergency of a "man of God." Amazingly, they immediately responded, handing the bag over to him. In minutes, it was in my hand. *A Kingdom sighting?* I think so!

Kingdom Seeing

As we noted above in the example of the Philippian jailor, Kingdom seeing can lead to Kingdom seeking. We usually do not seek what we have never seen (either in actuality or in our mind's eye). Kingdom seeing includes paying attention to God's truths until we "get" them. For example, when we are in the midst of considering any idea or concept, and then suddenly understand its meaning or how it functions, we often say, "Oh, now I see!" or "Now I get it!" We are indicating that we have envisioned something or now have a clear conception of a truth, principle, or notion. Similarly, once a Kingdom sighting comes into our "eye gate" or flows into our "ear gate," we catch a glimpse or hear the sound of a present Kingdom reality. If we are open to it, our "seeing" prompts us to want to see more of the same and to understand what it is all about. What we are looking for, our physical eyes can never see. The eternal spiritual realities of the Kingdom of God can be revealed and verified only by the Spirit of God to the spirit of man. Then we will "see," as in "I get it!"

I have been studying the Kingdom seriously and intensively for almost two decades, and I have been helplessly conquered by the King and His Kingdom. However, I didn't begin to earnestly seek the Kingdom until I "saw" it. What I saw initially was perhaps comparatively small, like *"a cloud as small as a man's hand"* (1 Kings 18:44), not much more than a fleeting thought. It now seems rather miniscule, because I have seen so much more since then. However, it was enough to make me want to see more. As soon as I saw the reality of it, I sought it. And my desire to see and to seek the Kingdom continues to grow exponentially!

> I didn't begin to earnestly seek the Kingdom
> until I "saw" it.

For me, Kingdom sightings are more frequent now than they have ever been, and I am sure it is because I am looking for them, expecting to see them. When I understood the concept of Kingdom sightings, I began to keep alert to their presence and to detect evidences of the Kingdom in many areas of my life. The following story demonstrates how I came to "see" a principle of prayer in relation to experiencing a Kingdom sighting.

When I was growing up, my family was prone to bronchial problems, mainly asthma. My siblings developed signs of asthma as small children, while I was somehow asthma-free. As they got older, they seemed to outgrow the disorder, while I grew into it! It was not a life-threatening condition, but it was somewhat bothersome; it was highly inconvenient and a hindrance to my sleep. I was dependent on a small spray container of asthma medicine with the trade name Asthmanefrin. It was so effective that it would take only moments after I had breathed a few whiffs of the spray for the symptoms to be relieved. I accepted this condition and lived with it, but I have since found that we often miss miracles by our own faulty reasoning, such as "It's not serious, so why bother to pray about it?" Please accept this axiom: *No disorder is too small (or too large) to exclude the element of heaven's touch!*

When I was writing my book *Much More*, I discussed many of the privileges we should enjoy as Christians. One of those chapters was on the "much more" of faith. As I dealt with the subject, I was experiencing an asthmatic attack. Suddenly, I had the distinct impression that God was saying to me, "I want to heal you of your asthma." Frankly, I was so surprised that this impression was so clear and persistent that I laid my work aside and began to internally inquire of the Lord how this might take place.

When I first heard this message from the Father about His desire to heal me, I thought, *That's very good, I would like that.* But nothing happened. Then His still, small voice within me seemed to say, *The key to this matter is your faith.* (Remember, that was the subject of the chapter I was involved in writing.) My interest took an excited leap as I awaited the next stage in this mini-drama.

Now I heard the Lord say, *You must believe that I **want** to heal you.* My answer was quick, *Yes, Lord, I believe You want to heal me!* Still nothing happened; my asthma continued unrelieved.

The next thing I heard was, *You must believe more than that; you must believe that I **can** heal you.* My answer was immediate, *Yes, Lord, I believe You can.* Again, nothing noticeable happened. The fact is, my heavy wheezing (the major symptom of asthma) continued to intensify. Then I received yet another message from the Lord: *There's still more you need to believe; you need to believe that I **will**.* For the third time, I agreed and declared my belief, *Lord, I believe You will!* Still no change in the asthma attack.

I was surprised at what I heard after that: *You must yet believe one more thing—that I **have healed** you.* Hearing this, my first thought was rather flippant: *I'd be glad to believe that You have healed me when You do heal me.* But at the end of that thought, I was suddenly reminded of Mark 11:24, which reads,

> *Therefore I tell you, all the things you pray and ask for—believe that you **have received them**, and you will have them.*

I am sure I had read this truth before because I had previously memorized Mark 11:24, but it had not registered within me to the extent that it now did. I must receive, and then I will have! Wow! I had missed that one vital component to faith. Readily and happily, I blurted out, "Lord, I believe You have healed me. Thank You very much! I am healed!" The only problem was that the asthma attack persisted, and perhaps even worsened a bit.

I finished my writing for the night and prepared for bed, still wheezing and taking shallow, labored breaths. As I repeated, almost under my breath, "I am healed," my confidence began to fade. At the nightstand, I reached for the little vial of medicine that could give me relief after just a couple of whiffs, but I was instantly arrested by the question, *If you are healed, why are you reaching for the medicine?* I gave a weak answer about maybe using it in case I might need it. The Lord would have none of it! The battle of faith was on. I put the medicine back on the nightstand, out of reach, and went to bed, wheezing and whispering softly, "Praise the Lord, I am healed." Then I pulled the covers up and prepared for a fitful night's sleep. As I repeated giving thanks for my healing, I dozed off, only to be interrupted every few minutes by the wheezing. This continued for several hours; I would experience a few minutes of sleep, then I would wake up, fighting for breath and stubbornly thanking God for my healing. Before you accuse me of foolishness and presumption, read what happened next: I awakened the following morning breathing clearly, and I have never had asthma since! That event took place more than forty years ago.

I didn't know what to call it then, but I now know that my healing was a true Kingdom sighting. Remember that a Kingdom sighting is a visible happening, a received word, or an inner revision of one's emotions or thought patterns that can be explained only as a heavenly invasion into our world. The Kingdom sighting of my healing came when I "saw" the truth of Mark 11:24. Thus, when we have a scriptural promise regarding prayer, we need to be intentional about applying it. I have almost completely gotten over being surprised when God answers a prayer immediately. In prayer, when we repeat to God one of His own, clear promises, we are also reminding our "inner man" of biblical truth and giving notice that we believe it.

We should realize that although prayer certainly moves God, when we develop an anticipation that the things we ask for will happen, God sometimes seems to wait to answer our prayer in order to strengthen our faith and to clarify His methods of answering. At other times, He seems delighted to answer right away. We simply need to swing to the rhythms of God's providences. In this light, one of my favorite and most oft-used Scriptures on prayer is 1 John 5:14–15:

> Now this is the confidence we have before Him: whenever we ask any-thing according to His will, He hears us. And if we know that He hears whatever we ask, **we know that we have what we have asked Him for.**

Here is another example of a Kingdom sighting due to prayer where there was an immediate answer. During a ministry trip to a particular state that included couples' con_____ _____ _____ ___ ___tual sons and daughters,

a_____   ual daughter was suffer-
i_____   -out disorder that often
i_____   including this woman,
a_____   r, and the pain level was
i_____   that she had no pain at
a_____   were drying up. By the
t_____   was that there was still
n_____   report, the healing was
c_____

K_____

_____ _____ _____ ____Kingdom, we will want
to_____ncy the more we under-
stand it and recognize its manifestations. Thus, seeing precedes seeking, and seeking results in more seeing. But our seeking has to be of a certain character. If we think we must have certain feelings or satisfying explana-tions to see a Kingdom manifestation, we may die disappointed. It is signif-icant that, with both His words and His actions, Jesus made clear that as we seek the Kingdom, we need qualities similar to those of little children. This feature must not be overlooked in our pursuit of the Kingdom of God.

Apparently, it was of ultimate significance to Jesus that His followers understand the value of a childlike spirit in His Kingdom. His emphasis on childlikeness was obvious not only in His tender treatment of children but also in His rather shocking declarations recorded in all three Synoptic gospels, Matthew, Mark, and Luke:

> *At that time the disciples came to Jesus and said, "Who is greatest in the Kingdom of heaven?" Then He called a child to Him and had him stand among them. "I assure you," He said, "unless you are converted and become like children, you will never enter the Kingdom of heaven. Therefore, whoever humbles himself like this child—this one is the greatest in the Kingdom of heaven. And whoever welcomes one child like this in My name welcomes Me. But whoever causes the downfall of one of these little ones who believe in Me—it would be better for him if a heavy millstone were hung around his neck and he were drowned in the depths of the sea!"* (Matthew 18:1–6)

> *Then they came to Capernaum. When [Jesus] was in the house, He asked them, "What were you arguing about on the way?" But they were silent, because on the way they had been arguing with one another about who was the greatest. Sitting down, He called the Twelve and said to them, "If anyone wants to be first, he must be last of all and servant of all." Then He took a child, had him stand among them, and taking him in His arms, He said to them, "Whoever welcomes one little child such as this in My name welcomes Me. And whoever welcomes Me does not welcome me, but Him who sent Me."* (Mark 9:33–37)

> *Some people were bringing little children to Him so He might touch them, but His disciples rebuked them. When Jesus saw it, He was indignant and said to them, "Let the little children come to Me. Don't stop them, for the Kingdom of God belongs to such as these. I assure you: Whoever does not welcome the Kingdom of God like a little child will never enter it." After taking them in His arms, He laid His hands on them and blessed them.* (Mark 10:13–16)

> *Then an argument started among them about who would be the greatest of them. But Jesus, knowing the thoughts of their hearts, took a little child and had him stand next to Him. He told them, "Whoever*

welcomes this little child in My name welcomes Me. And whoever welcomes Me welcomes Him who sent Me. For whoever is least among you—this one is great. (Luke 9:46–48)

Why is it that we need to become like a child in order to enter the Kingdom? It is because a little child has no agenda, has not yet learned to be double-minded, is innocent, and is often naïve. A child therefore reaches out gladly to take the Kingdom.

Here are some ways we can approach our search for the Kingdom as a little child.

With humility. Much of the time, children are characterized by an unconscious humility. Observing such may prove a lesson much needed in adulthood! I heard someone describe an individual whose behavior was noticeably selfless and commendable in the following way: "He hasn't heard of himself yet!" We must bow both head and heart in order to enter God's Kingdom. Earthly humility points the way and paves the path to the heavenly Kingdom.

> *Exercising childlike trust is the trait of the overcomer.*

With trust. Suspicion is a learned trait, and it sabotages faith. Lack of trust also weakens the will and undermines proper thinking. In contrast, trust is a lifeline to continued and normal progress—spiritually, mentally and emotionally. Exercising childlike trust is the trait of the overcomer. We may risk naiveté, but it may prove worth the risk!

With openness to learning. We must be able to live comfortably with a deeply-felt consciousness of our own spiritual ignorance—and never stop learning. This is the launch pad to a lifetime of seeking God's ways. Ceasing to learn is a decision that declares, "I know all I need to know. Don't try to teach me; I'm all right!" Yet, ten million years from now (if eternity could be measured in time), we will still be ~~seeking the unsearchable realm of ultimate reality and cosmic infinity,~~ and the boundless mysteries of Father, Son, and Spirit. Thus, childlikeness is the lubrication that keeps the wheels of our ~~teachability and wisdom~~ turning.

With love. Most little children do not need to be taught the psychological and physiological benefits of receiving and giving love. They instinctively return the love that is offered to them, with immediacy and excitement. Put children amid a culture of love, and love will be multiplied in their lives by imitation. After being immersed in such an atmosphere, it is unlikely that they will grow up with a deficiency of love. Similarly, seeking the Kingdom involves wholeheartedly accepting God's love and forgiveness toward us, and giving our love to Him—as well as extending love to other people—because love is the nature of the King and His Kingdom.

With resilience regarding obedience. Children can be remarkably resilient in terms of being able to behave obediently after having been disciplined. In years regrettably long gone, my wife and I would entertain our grandchildren for a week at the beach. We called our place "Shalom by the Sea." Each grandchild was a study in changing moods, reactions, and responses to discipline. Thankfully, their grandmother and I were able to recall procedures of love, kindness, and firmness that had defused many explosive situations in their parents' lives when they were that age. Significantly, no matter how far the grandchildren's actions ventured from proper community behavior, their conduct always returned to normal. We called this propensity *resilience*—the ability to "fess up," settle down, and regain healthy relationships. *Resilience* is big word for little children, so we demonstrated it to them by taking a Ping-Pong ball and trying to keep it underwater, only to show that once we let it go, it would burst through the surface and bounce back. Such resilience is a prime trait of a healthy child (and, for that matter, a healthy adult) that should never be discarded, misplaced, or forgotten in adulthood.

With unself-consciousness. Unself-conscious behavior is beautiful to behold and is a trait that is perfected only in Kingdom culture. At the memorial service of a deeply respected and highly valued friend, I said, "He was a friend who didn't think of himself much.... He was too busy thinking of you and me."

Knowing the value of childlikeness for seeking the Kingdom, let us pray, "Father, in my Kingdom journey, let me recover some of the things I have lost in the transition from childhood to adulthood. Make me like a child again!"

Kingdom Seizing and Being Seized by the Kingdom

When we begin to see and to seek the Kingdom, we will be moved to *seize* what we have seen. About that time, what we have reached out to seize (the Kingdom), will instead seize us! What we have sought to apprehend, will apprehend us. I want to avoid presenting this in too simplistic a manner and thus risk losing the full impact of its truth. But it is, in fact, rather simple. First we *see*, then we *seek*—increasingly. As we *seek*, we simultaneously *seize* the Kingdom and are *seized* by it.

The best way I know to illustrate this concept is by the following almost cryptic testimony of the apostle Paul:

> *Not that I have already reached the goal or am already fully mature, but I make every effort to take hold of it because I also have been taken hold of by Christ Jesus.* (Philippians 3:12)

Paul had taken hold of (seized) Christ by faith, knowing that simultaneously Christ had taken hold of (seized) him. The tenacious belief that we have taken hold of Christ and have also been taken hold of by Him is a healing balm all along the way. And, as we discover more of Kingdom reality, we are bound to experience a rushing passion to seize more of the Kingdom, only to find that in our seizure of the Kingdom, we have been thoroughly apprehended by it. It gets us; we get it. Now we truly know Jesus as our Savior, Lord, and King.

Kingdom Speaking and Kingdom Sounding

What happens when we have seen the Kingdom, earnestly sought it, seized it, and been seized by it, all the while experiencing Kingdom sightings? We will share it through our lives and through our faculties, mainly by means of the raw, invisible power of the Spirit. But we will also engage in Kingdom *speaking*, articulating for ourselves and others the basics of the Kingdom. And we will take part in Kingdom *soundings*, the proclamation of the Kingdom for the world to hear. God will support these soundings with manifestations, demonstrating the reality of His Kingdom and the truth of the gospel, as occurred with Jesus' disciples:

> Then [Jesus] *said to them, "Go into all the world and preach the gospel to the whole creation." …And they went out and preached everywhere, the Lord working with them and* **confirming the word by the accompanying signs.** (Mark 16:15, 20)

Kingdom Searching and Kingdom Soaring

Seeking God's Kingdom will lead to Kingdom *searching*—a quest to discover even more of this grand realm. As we seek, we will find more than enough to make us want to keep looking for more. To seek the Kingdom is to find the Kingdom. To find the Kingdom is to find everything: God the Father, God the Son, and God the Holy Spirit. Continued seeking will result in continued finding, that is, continued delving into the unsearchable riches of the Trinity. I love that word *unsearchable*! It challenges any attempt to quantify God and His resources. There are no limits to Kingdom searching, which, as I wrote earlier, we will enjoy throughout eternity.

Are you getting into the swing of the dance? Are you waltzing with the adventure of seeking the Kingdom, moving in a new lifestyle that mirrors that of our King? Seeking does require energy, but results will begin to flow as the "law of exponentiality" (a brand-new term I coined) begins to manifest, with rapid growth or "super-multiplication" of Kingdom sightings and Kingdom living.

Finally, Kingdom sightings and all the rest of the steps we have reviewed will result in Kingdom *soaring*, or living continuously in the atmosphere of the Kingdom, where all things are possible.

The eternal Kingdom is our ultimate destination and focus, but the Kingdom is also on earth, and we find rest and refreshment along the way through Kingdom sightings, seeing, seeking, seizing, being seized, speaking, sounding, searching, and soaring. You can live in the realm of God's limitless Kingdom, where there are no borders, no horizons, no yesterdays, no tomorrows, no waiting, no weeping over the past, no worrying over the future—just living in one eternal *now* in the family of God.

Before you call me a mindless dreamer, remember that we are encouraged by Jesus to "*seek first the Kingdom of God and His righteousness, and all these things will be provided for you*" (Matthew 6:33). Permit me to link the above passage with the following:

> *So I say to you, keep asking, and it will be given to you. Keep searching, and you will find. Keep knocking, and the door will be opened to you. For everyone who asks receives, and the one who searches finds, and to the one who knocks, the door will be opened.* (Luke 11:9–10)

The seeking is never over, the finding never ceases, the journey never ends, and the glory of God never dims. As the familiar song goes, "That's the story of, that's the glory of *love.*"[20]

Using the words we have surveyed as markers along the way, I encourage you to journal your own Kingdom *sightings, seeing, seeking, seizing, being seized, searching, speaking, sounding,* and *soaring*—and *more!* There is always more in the Kingdom.

Seeking God's Righteousness

We have one more aspect of Matthew 6:33 to discuss in regard to seeking the Kingdom: "*…and His righteousness.*" To seek the Kingdom of God is to seek the God of the Kingdom. One of His Old Testament names is Jehovah-Tsidkenu, meaning "God our Righteousness."

> *In His days Judah will be saved, and Israel will dwell securely. This is what He will be named: Yahweh [the Lord] Our Righteousness.*
> (Jeremiah 23:6)

---

20. Billy Hill, "The Glory of Love," 1935. Emphasis added.

To seek the Kingdom first is also to seek righteousness first, because righteousness is God's nature, and therefore the lifestyle of the Kingdom is righteous. Note that the righteousness we are to seek is God's righteousness, not our own. The fact is, as we find His righteousness, we find ours in Him. The psalmists had it right:

Your throne, God, is forever and ever; the scepter of Your Kingdom is a scepter of justice. You love righteousness and hate wickedness.
(Psalm 45:6–7)

The heavens proclaim His righteousness, for God is the Judge.
(Psalm 50:6)

Then people will say, "Yes, there is a reward for the righteous! There is a God who judges on earth!" (Psalm 58:11)

My mouth will tell about Your righteousness and Your salvation all day long, though I cannot sum them up. I come because of the mighty acts of the Lord GOD; I will proclaim Your righteousness, Yours alone.
(Psalm 71:15–16)

My lips will shout for joy when I sing praise to You because You have redeemed me. Therefore, my tongue will proclaim your righteousness all day long.... (Psalm 71:23–24)

God, give Your justice to the king and Your righteousness to the king's son. He will judge Your people with righteousness and Your afflicted ones with justice. May the mountains bring prosperity to the people and the hills, righteousness. (Psalm 72:1–3)

In the New Testament, it becomes clear that Jesus is the source of our righteousness, and the gospel proclaims that righteousness.

For I am not ashamed of the gospel, because it is God's power for salvation to everyone who believes, first to the Jew, and also to the Greek.

For in it God's righteousness is revealed from faith to faith, just as it is written: The righteous will live by faith. (Romans 1:16–17)

But it is from Him that you are in Christ Jesus, who became God-given wisdom for us—our righteousness, sanctification, and redemption, in order that, as it is written: The one who boasts must boast in the Lord. (1 Corinthians 1:30–31)

It is time for us to commit the remainder of our lives to the priority of earnestly seeking and finding God's Kingdom and His righteousness.

10

KINGDOM SHAKING

I awakened this morning under a strange sense of destiny regarding this chapter and others to follow. Read it slowly and deliberately, stopping every now and again to review what you have read most recently.

> Yet once more I will shake not only the earth but also heaven. This expression, "Yet once more," indicates the removal of what can be shaken—that is, created things—so that what is not shaken might remain. Therefore, since we are receiving a Kingdom that cannot be shaken, let us hold on to grace. (Hebrews 12:26–28)

It's important to discern what is happening around us in our turbulent times so that we know how to respond to it. We know that Satan, with his kingdom of darkness, is continually trying to disrupt God's kingdom of light, and that we need to fight back in spiritual warfare. Yet there is another significant factor to the turbulence we are experiencing, which we began to explore in the chapter "The Coming Recovery": in the midst of a world inflicted by sin, sickness, and Satanic attack, there is a worldwide shaking of the nations and institutions of the world.

Whatever is happening on earth at this present throbbing moment, it may be best summarized in a secular song from an earlier generation: "Whole Lot of Shakin' Going On." I am not particularly fond of this song and its lyrics. However, the title endures in my mind when I survey the landscape of the world as I view it.

Today, terrorism and senseless killings seem to be daily occurrences, there are riots in the streets, political enmity abounds, and marriages are breaking apart. Thousands of lives are being offered as sacrifices to the gods of violence, with senseless murders and mutilations becoming commonplace in the news. No place in the world appears to be safe, while common sense and humane behavior are disappearing. Nature itself seems to be responding with turbulences, including earthquakes, typhoons, tornadoes, floods, tsunamis, volcanic eruptions, and pestilences.

It may be debatable whether the present unrest, violence, and devastation are the worst this old planet has ever endured. Yet we can all agree that there has never been a time when people were made aware of unrest more immediately and continuously than in these early years of the twenty-first century. Advances in communication guarantee that images of incidents all over the globe, wherever they are or whatever they are about—a civil war in Syria, a suicide bombing in Turkey, a mass murder in Oregon, the beheading of Christians in the Middle East, an earthquake in China, the destruction of hurricane flooding in Haiti—will pour with nauseating swiftness out of our television sets, our computers screens, or our smart phones into our lives in a tsunami of unspeakable sights, producing reactions of anxiety, fear, and despair.

We need not deny the present shaking, nor do we need to be discouraged because of it. As believers, we are afforded an eternal perspective that can liberate us from depression and lead us to hope and even anticipation. From where may we expect to see hope appear amid this global culture of fear and terror, this shaking of earthly kingdoms?

Let this shaking, on whatever level we experience it—personal, local, national, or global—turn us toward God's Kingdom. Remember, having always existed in God, the Kingdom is eternal. Having come to earth in Jesus Christ, the Kingdom is here. Being here, it offers a realm of righteousness, peace, and joy that will never end. Thus, our ascending hope is in God's eternal rule on earth.

Questions About the Shaking in Our World

This chapter will explore the following questions about the shaking we are experiencing:

1. What in the world is going on?

2. Who is behind the shaking?

3. What is the central issue of the shaking?

4. What is the message of the shaking?

5. What must we to do in response to the shaking?

My deep conviction is that if we can receive the answers to these questions and bow to the prospects delivered to us in Scripture, it will prove transformative in our lives and enable us to welcome God's Kingdom to earth. We will be on the cusp of the greatest season in human history!

You may have noticed that I am assuming, as well as asserting, that the shaking we are experiencing is traceable as to source, undeniable as to purpose, and transparent as to what we as believers should do about it. Accordingly, the title of this chapter, "Kingdom Shaking," is both intentional and vital because of this fact: *this shaking of earthly kingdoms is Kingdom in nature.*

1. What in the World Is Going On?

Every realm of life and every continent on earth is being shaken. This is not a simple case of mild turbulence, but severe upheaval. There is no place in the world where we can escape it; everyone is experiencing it. Although, to a degree, the upheaval I have been describing is not new and has occurred throughout human history, the measure of its intensity seems unparalleled, and it appears to be rapidly accelerating. Bad news seems to be followed by even worse news, so that we are prone to ask, "What does this all mean?"

Thinking people want to know the news behind the news—what is really going on in our society and world. Only the Bible has a proper handle on this. I have previously expressed that there are certain biblical passages that, while containing a clear message of hope for a particular people in a time of great stress and conflict, are freighted with such powerful truths that they are pertinent and helpful for people of all times and seasons. There is such a passage in Hebrews 12. It concerns a great shaking that seems so applicable to our current world crisis that it deserves our serious attention.

Again, one of the greatest truths about the Bible is its continuous relevance across the centuries. Because the Bible is the construct of God's eternal Spirit, the fruit of His life in us is borne on the sounds of God's voice in every age. The amazing timelessness and timeliness of God's Word guarantees guiding light for every succeeding generation. It is no less pertinent to the present generation than it was to the original one. As Paul wrote to the Corinthian believers about the example of the ancient Israelites in the wilderness:

> Now these things happened to them as examples, and they were written as a warning to us, on whom the ends of the ages have come.
> (1 Corinthians 10:11)

On this basis, let us take ownership of the eternal truths of God's Word for this present shaking. It is clear that Hebrews was written to and for a people who were caught in times of great frustration, distress, and chaos. Yet the book is filled with hope and certainty as few documents ever written. And perhaps as no other passage in the entire Bible, Hebrews 12:25–29 demonstrates that the faithfulness of God, the permanence of His covenant, the power of His Word, and the centrality and supremacy of Jesus Christ form an unparalleled source of undying confidence for those who have placed their faith in the Lord. This brief passage remains a dynamic template that, when laid over God's people in any and every age, will surely result in hope amid despair, joy amid brokenness, and light in the deepest darkness.

So let us now examine in full this precious passage of truth, keeping in mind our current world conditions and hearing what God has to say to us concerning them.

> *Make sure that you do not reject the One who speaks. For if they* [the Israelites at Mount Sinai] *did not escape when they rejected Him who*

warned them on earth, even less will we if we turn away from Him who warns us from heaven. His voice shook the earth at that time, but now He has promised, Yet ~~once more I will shake not only the earth but also heaven~~. This expression, "Yet once more," indicates the removal of what can be shaken—that is, created things—so that what is not shaken might remain. Therefore, since we are receiving a Kingdom that cannot be shaken, let us hold on to grace. By it, we may serve God acceptably, with reverence and awe, for our God is a consuming fire.

(Hebrews 12:25–29)

What is the meaning of this passage in particular, and the whole book of Hebrews in general?

- ◆ First and foremost, it is a message of hope centered on the work of Jesus Christ as dying Savior and living Lord.

- ◆ It is a clear and graphic re-centering of the gospel of hope in Jesus Christ.

- ◆ It is a review of the riches made available to us through what Jesus accomplished in His life, death, and resurrection and in His indwelling in the life of the believer.

- ◆ It is a source of hope and peace to people who have been traumatized by the world and find themselves in conditions marked by devastation and deficiency.

I suggest that you take a few minutes to slowly reread every word of the above passage, with the intention of noting its thought patterns and then interacting with it as we progress.

2. Who Is Behind the Shaking?

We should repeatedly ask this vital question amid every expression of turbulence in our lives, whether personal or corporate. Our well-being and mental peace rest on our answer, which determines the nature of our philosophy of life and how we live out our faith. I believe the best answer comes directly from this passage in Hebrews. The One behind the shaking is the One who is speaking, and the One who is speaking is doubtlessly none other than God!

Please understand that I am not saying God causes pain and suffering. He does not cause atrocities such as the Inquisition or the Holocaust, epidemics like the plague, or any of the current evils we are facing. I am saying that He remains sovereign through it all, continually working out His purposes in our fallen world. This may seem like deficient comfort to those who are seriously hurting, and to say that God is behind today's shaking may be hard to face. However, if you are angry or in despair because you are blaming this shaking on anybody or anything other than God, read on—this passage from Hebrews 12 can change your mind.

First note these phrases:

"...*the One who speaks*" (verse 25).

"...*who warned them on earth*" (verse 25).

"*His voice shook the earth...*" (verse 26).

Now read this full statement: "*His voice shook the earth at that time, but now He has promised, Yet once more I will shake not only the earth but also heaven*" (verse 26).

The peace that the Bible says believers are meant to experience (see for example, John 14:27) and that will "guard our hearts and minds in Christ Jesus" (see Philippians 4:7), awaits our determined decision to see God as the ruling power behind all things that happen. Again, God is not the cause of our pain but is sovereign over whomever or whatever is to blame, and He is continually with us to support us through everything we experience. I promise that if you will agree with this first fact, you will be on your way to a certain change of heart that will bring you peace at a new level.

Let me share some reassuring thoughts here about God's sovereign power. God never allows anything to happen that will not ultimately serve His purposes to receive glory for Himself and bring good to His children. Regardless of how hopeless, helpless, or desperate we may feel, the significance of anything that we are now going through is that God is in charge and will have His way. He will be glorified, and you and I will be better for it!

While addressing a Sunday morning crowd recently, I heard myself say the following: "I have very good news for you today. If you are a believer in, and follower of, Jesus Christ, everything that has happened to you, is happening to you, and will happen to you will work together to bring you to the highest expression of life in the universe. God, being God, and thus being in charge, will never allow anything to happen to you that will not, within the context of your obedience, bring great blessings to you, make you a better person, and bring glory to His name. Believing this perspective will make brief episodes of pain or discomfort more endurable, and distasteful events, disappointments, and great setbacks more valued. These words may initially seem dark and depressing, but you will soon discover that the brightest mornings follow the darkest nights, and the greatest blessings follow the greatest burdens."

> The righteous will be shaken toward God
> instead of away from Him.

When times are bad due to a nation's rebellion against God, both the wicked and the righteous of that nation will be affected by the shaking, but the righteous will be shaken *toward* God instead of away from Him. The template of hope in the believer's mind and the comfort of the Holy Spirit will bring islands of peace amid restless seas of confusion. The believer will find the strength to look past and beyond the present struggles and find hope that is ordinarily hidden from the unbeliever. Hope becomes brightest in the darkest experiences when we look to God instead of to things for our satisfaction and stability. Paul's prayer for the Roman believers is helpful for us in this regard: *"Now may the God of hope fill you with all joy and peace as you believe in Him so that you may overflow with hope by the power of the Holy Spirit"* (Romans 15:13).

Thus, the simple answer to question 2, without extensive theological discussion, is "God!" Coming like a song amid dark clouds are the words of the patriarch Joseph when he revealed his identity to his brothers, who had rejected him and sold him into slavery many years earlier. Joseph said, in effect, "It wasn't you but God who sent me here! You meant it for evil, but God meant it for good—and God won!" (See Genesis 50:20.)

3. What Is the Central Issue of the Shaking?

What is described as shaking the earth is the very voice of God. The words He speaks do more than convey information; they contain the power to affect the planet at every level. So the primary issue of the shaking is the Word (and words) of God. And the shaking is essentially the soundings and signs of the battle storm between the Kingdom of light and the kingdom of darkness.

4. What Is the Message of the Shaking?

We have seen that anything God initiates, as well as anything He allows, has a purpose. In times of shaking, it is helpful to be able to hear the particular message behind the shaking. It is the greatest medicine for hopelessness, and it prevents panic and even insanity. The answer to question 4, according to the passage in Hebrews, is crystal clear: "*This expression, 'Yet once more,' indicates the removal of what can be shaken—that is, created things—so that what is not shaken might remain*" (Hebrews 12:27).

First, the shaking is designed to expose "*what can be shaken*," and that involves "*created things*." This shaking is not just a threatening tremor but an announcement of the demise and removal of all that is superficial. And that, my friend, includes everything except the Kingdom and all that is in it! God's Kingdom alone is unshakable. Second, the shaking is designed to exalt what cannot be shaken. We are obliged to avoid trusting in the former and to have faith only in the latter!

5. What Should We Do in Response to the Shaking?

The last question addresses what this chapter is ultimately aiming at, and it clarifies the reasons behind the shaking. So, what should our response be? "Inquiring minds want to know" is the motto of a magazine not known for the truthfulness of its research, but the slogan is unquestionably true! You're going to love this answer, because applying it to your life immediately will yield instant results—from here to eternity. To your inquiring mind, allow the Scripture to speak for itself:

> *Therefore, since **we are receiving a Kingdom that cannot be shaken**, let us hold on to grace. By it, we may serve God acceptably, with reverence and awe.*   (Hebrews 12:28)

Please observe that the structure of the closing instruction is derived from the declaration *"we are receiving a Kingdom that cannot be shaken."* The indication is that included with such a reception of the Kingdom will be an accompanying "grip on grace," followed by acceptable, reverent worship. This is a passage about a Kingdom that cannot be shaken. Thus, the glad conclusion we may draw from any shaking we may be experiencing is that it is designed to bring about a decision on the part of those shaken to accept and embrace the Kingdom of God and to expect the gift of God's rule. No kingdom among humankind has ever been worthy of ultimate trust as God's eternal Kingdom is.

As we previously noted, the Kingdom was on the Creator's mind when He formed the first human beings and clearly stated their unchanging destiny:

> *God said, "Let us make man in Our image, according to Our likeness. **They will rule** the fish of the sea, the birds of the sky, the livestock, all the earth, and the creatures that crawl on the earth." So God created man in His own image; He created him in the image of God; He created them male and female. God blessed them, and God said to them, "Be fruitful, multiply, fill the earth, and **subdue** it. **Rule** the fish of the sea, the birds of the sky, and every creature that crawls on the earth."*
>   (Genesis 1:26–28)

Note the use of repetition in this passage by the writer, Moses, included to emphasize the significance of these words. In verse 26, Moses recorded God's stated intention that *"man"* rule over creation; in verse 27, he recorded the acts of God's deliberate creation of the man and the woman; in verse 28, he recorded God's commands to *"them"* (male and female) to rule, a repetition of His stated intentions. Most of the remainder of Genesis 1 is a remarkable list of what God gave Adam and Eve to rule over. This portion of Scripture concludes with, *"And it was so"*! (See Genesis 1:29–30.)

Moses then declared, *"God saw all that He had made, and it was **very** good"* (Genesis 1:31). I have included this verse and emphasized one of the words in it for a particular reason, which you may have missed. If so, it gives me great pleasure to point out that the phrase *"it was good"* was used six times previously in Genesis 1. (See verses 4, 10, 13, 18, 21, and 25.) However, in verse 31, Moses significantly included the word *"very."* The additional components since the last time *"it was good"* was used were the creation of Adam and Eve and the revelation of their rich inheritance, which surely merit the description *"very good"*!

> *This is a shaking toward renewed hope and purpose—that the human race will once more come under God's loving reign.*

God's unchanging purpose is that we were created with a command to reign over His whole creation, but as we have seen, our reign over God's creation is based on His reign over us. And that is the ultimate reason for the shaking we are experiencing in our world. This shaking is not only necessary and inevitable but also greatly encouraging because it is a shaking toward renewed hope and purpose—that the human race will once more come under God's loving reign. Until we see this, the shaking and every other apparently unfortunate earthly happening will seem like a tragedy instead of a blessing in disguise.

The passage in Hebrews we have been examining ends with this brief and bold declaration: *"For our God is a consuming fire"* (Hebrews 12:29).

This image opens a world of thinking regarding the nature of One who, as a fire, consumes sin but, at the same time, purifies the sinner. While God is love and light, He is also fire. And fire can variously reduce something to ashes, provide light in darkness, and bring warmth to a cold and threatening night. God can meet all needs, and He is filled with raw, unquenchable energy and undying passion.

Thus, the key factor in this season of shaking is not in discovering how to change the circumstances but in saying "Yes!" to the One who is behind the shaking, who alone is aware of what will remain unshakable, and who will one day give us a loving, lavish welcome into the eternal Kingdom of His dear Son. (See 2 Peter 1:11.) As this unfolds, the church will powerfully minister the gospel of the Kingdom in the world, with manifestations of hope, healing, and deliverance, demonstrating the love of Christ spiritually and materially to those who are in distress.

The hinge on which this whole passage swings is found in Hebrews 12:28: *"Therefore, since we are receiving a Kingdom that cannot be shaken…"*—the protocol and results of that act are crystal clear—*"…let us hold on to grace. By it, we may serve God acceptably, with reverence and awe."*

Here then, in review, are the five questions we have explored, their answers, and what they mean for us:

1. What in the world is going on? A Kingdom shaking. Therefore, we must sit up and take note.

2. Who is behind the shaking? God! We must recognize His sovereignty and thank Him in the midst of our circumstances.

3. What is central issue of the shaking? The Word (and words) of God. We need to listen to what God is saying and heed it.

4. What is message of the shaking? It identifies the Kingdom alone as unshakable. The Kingdom is the answer to life on earth and in eternity.

5. What should we do in response to the shaking? We must receive the unshakable Kingdom, hold on to God's grace, and worship God acceptably as we serve Him.

The strongest takeaway from this chapter is our mandated response to the shaking: *"receiving a Kingdom that cannot be shaken"* (Hebrews 12:28). At this point, I challenge you to respond by simply speaking the following prayer out loud:

Father, right now, not really knowing what all this means, I say, "I now receive the Kingdom as my continuing response to all that is happening!"

Now read this portion of the Hebrews passage again:

His voice shook the earth at that time, but now He has promised, Yet once more I will shake not only the earth but also heaven. This expression, "Yet once more," indicates the removal of what can be shaken— that is, created things—so that what is not shaken might remain.
(Hebrews 12:26–27)

Know that the shaking experienced in the displacement, dispersion, and exile of God's children in New Testament times will to some measure be the lot of His children today. That being so, we join with them in receiving this declaration:

Now may the God of peace, who brought up from the dead our Lord Jesus—the great Shepherd of the sheep—with the blood of the everlasting covenant, equip you with all that is good to do His will, working in us what is pleasing in His sight, through Jesus Christ. Glory belongs to Him forever and ever. Amen.
(Hebrews 13:20–21)

It is amazing how James Russell Lowell's grand and glorious poem, "The Present Crisis," written in the nineteenth century, fits our world today. The following are several of its stanzas.

Once to every man and nation comes the moment to decide,
In the strife of Truth with Falsehood, for the good or evil side;
Some great cause, God's new Messiah, offering each the bloom or blight,
Parts the goats upon the left hand, and the sheep upon the right,
And the choice goes by forever 'twixt that darkness and that light.

Hast thou chosen, O my people, on whose party thou shalt stand,
Ere the Doom from its worn sandals shakes the dust against our
land?
Though the cause of Evil prosper, yet 'tis Truth alone is strong,
And, albeit she wander outcast now, I see around her throng
Troops of beautiful, tall angels, to enshield her from all wrong.

Backward look across the ages and the beacon-moments see,
That, like peaks of some sunk continent, jut through Oblivion's
sea;
Not an ear in court or market for the low foreboding cry
Of those Crises, God's stern winnowers, from whose feet earth's
chaff must fly;
Never shows the choice momentous till the judgment hath passed
by.

Pay close attention to the next stanza:

Careless seems the great Avenger; history's pages but record
One death-grapple in the darkness 'twixt old systems and the
Word;
Truth forever on the scaffold, Wrong forever on the throne—
Yet that scaffold sways the future, and, behind the dim unknown,
Standeth God within the shadow, keeping watch above his own.

Here is the final stanza of the poem:

New occasions teach new duties; Time makes ancient good
uncouth;
They must upward still, and onward, who would keep abreast of
Truth;
Lo, before us gleam her camp-fires! we ourselves must Pilgrims be,
Launch our Mayflower, and steer boldly through the desperate
winter sea,
Nor attempt the Future's portal with the Past's blood-rusted key.[21]

---

21. James Russell Lowell, "The Present Crisis," 1844, http://www.bartleby.com/42/805.
html.

A Final Note on Shaking

The night I began writing this chapter was an evening of seemingly unprecedented shaking on the planet: the Middle East was an inferno of conflict as Israel and Gaza duked it out with rockets and airstrikes; Russia was threatening a full-scale invasion of the Ukraine; a violent terrorist army was marching across Iraq murdering, pillaging, mutilating, beheading, and threatening to kill all Christians who did not renounce faith in Christ and bow to Allah. All this was going on while the streets of a St. Louis, Missouri, suburb called Ferguson was flame with violent protest. The shaking has multiplied since then, and it is safe to assume that as you read this book, similar crises are occurring. The message of this chapter has never been more strategic than right now.

It became personally strategic for me later when I later sat down to do some serious rewriting of this chapter. I had begun the revisions after rising at 4:30 a.m., eager to write about hope amid the shaking. Suddenly, my heart device, installed several years earlier to monitor and revise irregular behavior of my heart, fired. I pray you never have to know how that experience feels, but it is best described as being similar to being kicked in the chest by a mule. Needless to say, the heavenly Father had my full attention. For minutes, I battled between faith and fear, reality and imagination. Drawing near to God was my immediate response, but fear and panic knocked at the door. Yet I had already written the following words, and it was a no-brainer to agree with them:

> Receiving the Kingdom amid the shaking is the master secret in this whole issue of Kingdom living!

My fear bowed to my faith, and my imagination yielded to God's reality. God reigns, and I live! It is no accident that the next chapter is about awe and astonishment!

Kingdom Mind-set Scriptures

I conclude this chapter with the following Scriptures about God's sovereignty and His provision for us. Please do not skim through them lightly;

if you read them carefully, they can powerfully soak your present mind-set in God's thought patterns so that it matches a Kingdom outlook. It will help to read them aloud. You will be glad you did!

> The LORD sits enthroned forever; He has established His throne for judgment. (Psalm 9:7)

> The LORD is King forever and ever; the nations will perish from His land. (Psalm 10:16)

> You reveal the path of life to me; in Your presence is abundant joy; in Your right hand are eternal pleasures. (Psalm 16:11)

> Lift up your heads, you gates! Rise up, ancient doors! Then the King of glory will come in. Who is He, this King of glory? The LORD of Hosts, He is the King of glory. (Psalm 24:9–10)

> The LORD is the strength of His people; He is a stronghold of salvation for His anointed. Save Your people, bless Your possession, shepherd them, and carry them forever. (Psalm 28:8–9)

> The LORD sat enthroned at the flood; the LORD sits enthroned, King forever. The LORD gives His people strength; the LORD blesses His people with peace. (Psalm 29:10–11)

> You turned my lament into dancing; You removed my sackcloth and clothed me with gladness, so that I can sing to You and not be silent. LORD my God, I will praise You forever. (Psalm 30:11–12)

> May Yahweh, the God of Israel, be praised from everlasting to everlasting. Amen and amen. (Psalm 41:13)

> Your throne, God, is forever and ever; the scepter of Your Kingdom is a scepter of justice. (Psalm 45:6)

Just as we heard, so we have seen in the city of Yahweh of Hosts, in the city of our God; God will establish it forever. (Psalm 48:8)

This God, our God forever and ever—He will always lead us.
(Psalm 48:14)

I am at rest in God alone; my salvation comes from Him. He alone is my rock and my salvation, my stronghold; I will never be shaken.
(Psalm 62:1–2)

May the LORD *God, the God of Israel, who alone does wonders, be praised. May His glorious name be praised forever; the whole earth is filled with His glory. Amen and amen.* (Psalm 72:18–19)

Who do I have in heaven but You? And I desire nothing on earth but You. My flesh and my heart may fail, but God is the strength of my heart, my portion forever. (Psalm 73:25–26)

I will sing about the LORD'*s faithful love forever; I will proclaim Your faithfulness to all generations with my mouth. For I will declare, "Faithful love is built up forever; You establish Your faithfulness in the heavens."* (Psalm 89:1–2)

Lord, You have been our refuge in every generation. Before the mountains were born, before You gave birth to the earth and the world, from eternity to eternity, You are God. (Psalm 90:1–2)

11

THE RETURN TO ASTONISHMENT

It has taken me a while to get to this point, but now that I am in my eighties, I am in the late chapters of my life. Aging has been given a fairly grim appraisal in contemporary society, and evidences abound that seem to confirm this view beyond argument. However, allow me, if you will, to give what appears to be a minority report: I, Jack Taylor, am an astonished and excited old man! At a time when I am supposed (they say) to settle down to a life of ease and retirement (that was actually twenty-some-odd years ago), here I am, with as much anticipation as a child on Christmas morning. Here's why.

Ever since Eden's tragedy, life on earth has not been easy. After a few beginning pages describing pristine beauty and bliss for the first inhabitants of the world, the Bible becomes a catalog of catastrophes for the human race, punctuated by brief episodes of peace. Yet in its final analysis and message, it provides the only hope for humanity's ability to cope with life.

But the message of the Bible does more than merely help us to hope and to cope. Within its pages, we find stunning promises of Kingdom truth that can completely transform our lives, personally and collectively, such as we discovered in the last chapter on "Kingdom Shaking." A simple survey of the scriptural record of past, present, and future will introduce us to a life of expectation and even *astonishment*. And this is the atmosphere in which I find myself living today.

I have found something better than the fountain of youth—it is not even a pill or a series of age-resistant treatments. I have discovered the Kingdom of God, the Big Picture, the Eternal Realm of the heavenly Father. I am more excited today than I was the first day I began to discover it. The more I learn, the more excited I become. The more I know, the more I am aware of what I don't know—and of how much more there is to know that I will soon know! The thrilling thought that assaults my mind is that, in a million years, when time has given way to eternity, we will still be discovering the reaches of the infinite mind of our Mighty God, His Spirit, and His Son!

> *In a million years, we will still be discovering the reaches of God's infinite mind.*

E. Stanley Jones was once writing one of his many books in a borrowed house. He took his eyes off his writing for a moment, looked up, and saw his image in a mirror in a room across the hall. He took the liberty to talk to himself, an acquired practice enjoyed mainly by old folks. Addressing himself to his image in the mirror, he observed, "Stanley Jones, you're a happy man, aren't you?" He then experienced an upgrade in the self-talking world by answering to himself, "That I am, that I am!" The dialogue continued, "Pray tell, Stanley Jones, can you tell the reason for your happiness?" Said Mr. Jones to Mr. Jones, "Well, yes, I can tell you. One day I was walking across a field and tripped over something. I looked down, and there was a chest. I opened it and found the Treasure, the Kingdom of God, and I've been huggin' myself ever since!"[22]

22. Paraphrased from a recorded sermon by E. Stanley Jones.

I had the opportunity to hear E. Stanley Jones preach, and I have read his books. Based on those, I have concluded that if happiness were a game, Jones would have won it by far; if happiness were a movie, he would have won an Oscar for his performance in it; if happiness were a hundred-yard dash, he would have finished in less than ten seconds flat! I think I know how he felt. I am happy and amazed, and it has to do with the King—who He is and what He has done, is doing, and will do. I am incurably optimistic, totally overwhelmed, shamelessly intrigued, and unapologetically astonished by the Kingdom.

During a recent preaching engagement, I said, "If you are not excited, you just don't understand the situation." I was not talking about the situations that scream from the newspaper headlines or the grim reports of the television news shows about our wide world with its pains and sorrows. I was talking about the *real* news, not the overt news. I was talking about the eternal, everlasting, all-consuming, ultimate good news, the gospel of the Kingdom.

Yes, I am astonished about the Kingdom!

I am astonished that there really is such a God as ours. If there weren't such a God as He, I would remark, "Well, there certainly ought to be!" But, hallelujah, there is one!

I am astonished that this God is the CEO of the largest enterprise in the universe, the Kingdom; in fact, it's so huge that it includes the universe!

I am astonished that God established His eternal Kingdom on earth and called Himself a Father with a Family Business that will never fail, and that His Kingdom, even at this present moment, rules over all. (See Psalm 103:19.)

I am astonished that this God, the Creator and Sustainer of the entire universe, encompassing all that is, would take an interest in His creation in general, in humankind in particular, and in you and me specifically.

I am astonished about our God's response to humanity. The first human beings totally and thoroughly fell, plunging all their successors into open rebellion against their Creator. But God, although forced to remove Adam and Eve from their garden home, never ceased His stubborn pursuit of His errant children. He maintained His purposes for humanity and ultimately brought Someone into view called the second Adam, sending Him into the game of life as our Substitute. This Someone died *for* us, *as* us, and *with* us, and was resurrected to live *in* us.

I am astonished that God not only gave His own Son to pay the penalty that sin demanded, but also arranged for His Son, in the person of the Holy Spirit, to enter my redeemed humanity and make me a citizen of His own eternal Kingdom. This gives me—and all who belong to Him—the right to live and love victoriously here on earth and to share His eternal rule over the cosmos forever and ever.

I am astonished that over seventy years ago, a bashful and backward country kid was prompted by the Holy Spirit to give his life to Jesus, making him a child of the heavenly family with joint ownership in the Family Business. (I didn't know then that I was part of the Family Business, but I know it now!) I was also made an apprentice, training for reigning over the universe in eternity.

I am astonished that I—along with every other believer—hold stock in God's Family Business. Better than that, I am an equal heir—with Jesus and all believers—of God's limitless riches now and forever.

I am astonished that this God has committed Himself to my eternal well-being and continues to exercise His care, calling His legions of angels to assist, comfort, and encourage me, holding me in their hands lest I stub my toe, warding off demonic attacks. (See Psalm 91:11–14.)

I am astonished that God, indwelling me by His Spirit, pursues His eternal purpose in and through me.

I am astonished that God has given His children faith and prayer, the currency of His Kingdom, to draw on His limitless resources, which will never fail.

I am astonished at what God has done in the past, what He is doing at this present moment, and what He will do in the future to move all creation everywhere under His blessed, eternal, and unopposed dominion.

I am astonished that this God sits on His throne, confidently ruling over this vast universe, not walking around His throne with wringing hands and furrowed brow, worrying about the undertakings of Satan and his demons and their plans to unseat Him.

I am astonished that God knows my name and yours, and that, though knowing everything about us, He loves us still and leads us with perfect wisdom and unconditional love, loading us with expertise and limitless resources to become everything we were redeemed to be.

I am astonished that, knowing our past, present, and future, God is able to quiet the noisy, accusing past, remove the gnawing regret of sin, settle the uncertain and threatening future, and bring us peace as He speaks with authority over the turbulent waves of our lives, assuring us of certain safety.

I am astonished at the whole spiritual realm, replete with the radiance, majesty, and glory of Him who sits on the throne of the whole universe.

I am astonished that this God is eternal, infinite, ineffable, and timeless, and yet enters our narrow frame of time and gives us total accessibility to all of His unsearchable treasures.

I am astonished that God was and is and is to come; that there is no place where He is not; that there is no time in the past, present, or future when He ceases to be. He exists in every dimension—replete, complete, and the ultimate in every attribute. To Him and Him alone are the glory, the honor, and the power forever. God is:

+ Omnipresent (He is everywhere, both geographically and chronologically, in every time zone, area code, zip code, and individual heart.)

+ Omniscient (He knows everything about everything.)

+ Omnipotent (He can do anything about everything.)

+ Omni-benevolent (He loves us all with perfect love.)

I am astonished that God has breathed His words to and into holy men who wrote them down, compiling a Book that has survived and thrived throughout the millennia. Though fought over, raged at, plotted against, even wounded in the house of its friends, its very existence at times threatened by law, the Bible endures still, living up to its vaunted reputation and leaving a trail of healing, health, and wholeness. It still engenders fear and hostility in the hearts of heedless men. However, the attacks upon it through the ages, combined with its relentless sustainability to abide and thrive, are eloquent testimony of its authenticity.

I am astonished that the Bible is the distillation of the very breath of God, which leaps off its pages in life-giving power as the Holy Spirit gives it new breath and fresh dynamic in every generation. I am astonished that the sound of its words being read aloud has redeeming and healing power, changing the helpless and the hopeless into clarions of endless joy; transforming, for example, dreary, defeated alcoholics into loving fathers and faithful husbands, and wild demoniacs into sane and solid citizens.

> *The eternal realm of the Kingdom*
> *deserves our astonishment.*

I am astonished at the uncounted legions of angels who are sent from heaven's throne to gain continuous victories over the forces of darkness and to establish beachheads around the world for missional invasions of the gospel of the Kingdom. I am astonished at the passing estimates of the size of these armies of angels: *"Thousands upon thousands, and ten thousand times ten thousand"* (Revelation 5:11 NIV).

Astonished? Yes, helplessly and hopelessly astonished that this gospel of the Kingdom will be preached to every nation in one generation, and then the end will come!

I am astonished at all this and more! We can never say with wisdom, "It just doesn't get any better than this!" It does get better, and it will keep on getting better as the government of God continues, never ceasing in its increase and peace (see Isaiah 9:7 NKJV, KJV) until the kingdoms of this world become the Kingdom of our Lord and of His Christ (see Revelation

11:15). Then Jesus will completely rule everywhere and over everybody and everything forever and ever...and a thousand evers!

Yes, I am astonished! I am astonished! I am so astonished over all this that I pray and hope that you will become astonished over the King and His Kingdom, too. I offer this proposal: I would like to give you my own astonishment, which never fades in the giving. And my astonishment has not yet peaked! You can receive my astonishment as yours by faith until you can be as astonished as I am and walk out your own! Such action involves a present impartation. Take it now! Not later, but right now. Is it a deal? Declare your astonishment until you begin to sense it welling up within you. Then find a place to express your growing excitement. Your astonishment has only begun!

Please pause here and carefully review what you have just read. The eternal realm of the Kingdom deserves our astonishment. Don't wait until you are finished with this book to start feeling amazed. Astonishment is yours to receive right now! (Now honestly, don't you already feel just a little bit better?)

Finally, I am astonished that you and I are living in a season near the end of time as we know it, when the original gospel of the Kingdom is being sounded with stunning frequency and deepening continuity and understanding.

The Kingdom is a place of excitement and laughter! To get close to the King is to live close to laughter, because He is a laughing God, and with good reason: He knows the whole story, the entire course of the history of the universe, and particularly how human history will wind up and work out.

The One enthroned in heaven **laughs.** (Psalm 2:4)

Interestingly, the context of the above verse is humankind's rebellion against God and potential judgment, along with the opportunity of reconciliation with Him:

Why do the nations rebel and the peoples plot in vain? The kings of the earth take their stand, and the rulers conspire together against the

LORD and His Anointed One: *"Let us tear off their chains and free ourselves from their restraints." The One enthroned in heaven laughs; the Lord ridicules them. Then He speaks to them in His anger and terrifies them in His wrath: "I have consecrated My King on Zion, My holy mountain." I will declare the* LORD's *decree: He said to Me, "You are my Son; today I have become Your Father. Ask of me, and I will make the nations Your inheritance and the ends of the earth Your possession. You will break them with a rod of iron; You will shatter them like pottery." So now, kings, be wise, receive instruction, you judges of the earth. Serve the* LORD *with reverential **awe** and rejoice with trembling. Pay homage to the Son or He will be angry and you will perish in your rebellion, for His anger may ignite at any moment. All those who take refuge in Him are happy.*   (Psalm 2:1–12)

If you are still not astonished at this moment, don't go any further. Read the above passage again, preferably aloud. Are you there yet? I have personally read it three times during this writing, and I am more astonished than ever! I emphasized the word *"awe"* in the passage for this reason: I believe that astonishment is awe on steroids! The Kingdom of God calls for a fresh infusion of astonishment in the lives of individuals, and a full invasion globally. Receive it!

After suffering a debilitating heart attack, the great Jewish scholar Abraham Joshua Heschel told a friend, in effect, "Never once in my life did I ask God for success or wisdom or power or fame. I asked for wonder, and he gave it to me." Heschel also said,

> Awe is more than an emotion; it is a way of understanding, insight into a meaning greater than ourselves. The beginning of awe is wonder, and the beginning of wisdom is awe....
>
> ...Awe is a sense for the transcendence, for the reference everywhere to mystery beyond all things....
>
> Knowledge is fostered by curiosity; wisdom is fostered by awe. *Awe precedes faith; it is the root of faith.*[23]

---

23. Abraham J. Heschel, *Who Is Man?* (Stanford, CA: Stanford University Press, 1965), 88–89. Emphasis is in the original.

Conclusion

The word *conclusion* has a twofold meaning. First, it means the end of a matter, the point of termination. Second, it means a judgment someone has reached after giving a matter thought. On this basis, I cannot resist this most powerful *conclusion* to this chapter on astonishment: *"For the Kingdom of God is not eating and drinking, but righteousness, peace, and joy in the Holy Spirit* (Romans 14:17)!

12

THE KINGDOM AND
THE FATHER

J esus' central message was the Kingdom of God, and within this message He revealed a vital aspect of our relationship with God as King: He is not only our Ruler but also our Father. The church must reaffirm this message as part of the recovery of a Kingdom mentality, because God has always employed the family paradigm to advance His Kingdom on earth.

> The magnificent obsession of Jesus the Messiah is that all of humanity would know God as a Father.[24]

> I would want to maintain more strongly than ever that the only hope of the Church is in new openness to the Holy Spirit who brings us into living contact with the Father and the Son. The charismatic movement as a thing in itself may well be almost over, but the renewal of the Church by the Holy Spirit has only just begun.

---

24. Jim McNally, *Sonship: The Word Made Flesh* (Pasadena, CA: Harvest International Ministries, 2011), 1.

In that ongoing renewal our realised relationship to God the Father has a central and decisive part. It is both corrective and constructive, a source of confidence and of courage, of hope and of joy.[25]

If God had wanted something besides a family, He would have had us call Him something besides a Father.[26]

The Kingdom Paradigm of God the Father/God the Son

The Kingdom has everything to do with God as Father and Jesus as Son. God is likened to a Father several times in the Old Testament. One reference is in Isaiah 9:6 (NIV), where Jesus is referred to as *"Wonderful Counselor, Mighty God, Everlasting Father, Prince of Peace."* Another is in Psalm 2, which is a Messianic psalm containing this declaration from God:

> *"I have consecrated My King on Zion, My holy mountain." I will declare the* LORD'*s decree: He said to Me, "You are My Son; today I have become Your Father."* (Psalm 2:6–7)

What you have just read is one of the most remarkable legal decrees ever spoken in the universe. The Messianic declaration places the Father/Son issue right in the middle of the equation. This passage also shows us that even before God created the world, He was the Father. Before He spoke anything that was recorded in the Bible, He was the Father. He is eternally the Father. He never was not the Father. He will never not be the Father.

When God came to earth in the person of Jesus Christ, He personally taught and modeled for us the relational structure of the Kingdom, which is the Father/Son paradigm. Paul learned to model this relationship as he

---

25. Thomas A. Smail, *The Forgotten Father* (Eugene, OR: Wipf and Stock Publishers, 2001), 9–10.
26. A statement made by Andy Taylor, my biological nephew and spiritual son.

ministered to others. There is no way to measure the depth and intensity of the pathos in the apostle's heart when he wrote these words:

> I'm not writing this to shame you, but to warn you as my dear children. For you can have 10,000 instructors in Christ, but you can't have many fathers. For I became your father in Christ Jesus through the gospel. Therefore I urge you to imitate me. (1 Corinthians 4:14–16)

Paul was, I believe, laying the template of Kingdom and fatherhood (family) over the whole of his relationships. The Kingdom cannot fully function apart from the Father/Son component, nor was it established to function without it. Again, this paradigm is clearly expressed through the relationship between God the Father and Jesus Christ the Son. That being true, why should we ever expect the church to function properly apart from the template of the Kingdom and Fatherhood? Try as we might, we will not succeed in functioning as we were meant to until we imitate the relationship between the Father and the Son—in our own relationship with God and in our ministry to others.

The Fatherhood/Sonship Launching Pad

We begin to explore this theme of the Father/Son paradigm by seeing how it manifested in Jesus' relationship with the Father, and then Jesus' relationship with one of His spiritual sons, the apostle John. First, let's return to the scene of Jesus as a twelve-year-old when He stayed behind in Jerusalem to talk with the teachers in the temple. He told His worried earthly parents, Mary and Joseph, who had been looking for Him, "Why were you searching for Me?... Didn't you know that I had to be in My Father's house?" (Luke 2:49). Building on what we discussed earlier about this incident, we can see these significant aspects in Jesus' answer:

1. At twelve years of age, He knew that He was God's Son.

2. He knew that His purpose on earth was in the "house" of His Father. He had a filial relationship with God as His Son. This relationship would largely be kept secret for almost two decades. The Kingdom waited for the fullness of time for this revelation, which was released at Jesus' baptism

when God the Father said, "*This is My beloved Son. I take delight in Him!*" (Matthew 3:17). The same affirmation was given later in Jesus' ministry at His transfiguration. (See Matthew 17:5.)

Yet, as a human being, Jesus also had to train in Sonship while He was growing up. In His earlier years, He was no doubt a helper to his step-father, Joseph, in the carpenter shop, and later He probably became His father's apprentice and subsequently an accomplished carpenter. But much more than this, He was learning, in the context of a human family, both the high calling and protocol involved in being a good son—both to Joseph and to His Father in heaven.

We noted earlier that a different translation of Luke 2:49 reads, "*Why did you seek Me? Did you not know that I must be about My Father's business?*" (NKJV). This pursuit of His Father's "*business*" was constant and intense for the next eighteen years of His life prior to His ministry. Then, when Jesus declared, at the beginning of His ministry, that the Kingdom had come near, it was an inevitable utterance exploding from that Fatherhood/ Sonship launching pad.

Just as Jesus learned Sonship with the Father, He taught His disciples—and all of us—to think of God in terms of our Father. Significantly, He linked God's Fatherhood with the Kingdom, as in the following passages:

> *Therefore, you should pray like this: "**Our Father** in heaven, Your name be honored as holy. **Your Kingdom come**. Your will be done on earth as it is in heaven."* (Matthew 6:9–10)

> *Don't be afraid, little flock, because **your Father** delights to give you **the Kingdom**.* (Luke 12:32)

Thus, the Kingdom is all about the Father/Son relationship and the Kingdom family of God. The greatest thing about God is that He is the Father of Jesus Christ. The greatest thing about Jesus is that He is the Son of God the Father. And the Holy Spirit is the Spirit of the Father and of the Son.

The Disciple Whom Jesus Loved

Nowhere in Scripture are we welcomed into the depth of the intimacies between God the Father and Jesus Christ the Son than in the gospel of John. Amid many other emphases, this book heartily reveals the dynamics of the relationship and life-flow between Them. I suggest that you reread this gospel, highlighting the words "Father" and "Son." The number of times these words are mentioned is significant indeed. Jesus refers to God as Father over a hundred times, and to Himself as Son over sixty times.

> *In the gospel of John, Jesus refers to God as Father over a hundred times.*

John seems to habitually lean close to Jesus; He was evidently an admiring "Jesus watcher," and perhaps this is why he was able to best chronicle, as no other New Testament author, this greatest relationship in the universe. And that is not all. In his first two epistles, still staggering under the blessed weight of the astounding revelation of the Father/Son paradigm, John mentions the Father sixteen times and Jesus as Son twenty-six times. He even refers to himself as the "disciple whom Jesus loved," and he was apparently never censured for saying that. John had discovered, perhaps to a measure beyond every other disciple, the love relationship between Father and Son and thus began to confess a fact he deeply felt. It may well have been that he felt such a love for Jesus, the Father, and the Spirit that the depth and intimacy of their relationship penetrated everything about which he thought and wrote.

The following are the four places in his gospel where he spoke of himself in the third person as "the disciple Jesus loved":

*When Jesus saw his mother and **the disciple He loved**, standing there, He said to His mother "Woman, here is your son." Then he said to the disciple, "Here is your mother." And from that hour the disciple took her into his home.* (John 19:26–27)

*On the first day of the week Mary Magdalene came to the tomb early, while it was still dark. She saw that the stone had been removed from the tomb. So she ran to Simon Peter and to the other disciple, **the one Jesus loved**, and said to them, "They have taken the Lord out of the tomb, and we don't know where they have put Him!"* (John 20:1–2)

*"Cast the net on the right side of the boat," [Jesus] told them, "and you'll find some [fish]." So they did, and they were unable to haul it in because of the large number of fish. **The disciple, the one Jesus loved**, said to Peter, "It is the Lord!"* (John 21:6–7)

*Peter turned around and saw **the disciple Jesus loved** following them. That disciple was the one who had leaned back against Jesus at the supper and asked, "Lord, who is the one that's going to betray You?"* (John 21:20)

The idea of John's special closeness to Jesus is strengthened by the fact that when Jesus was dying on the cross, He committed His mother, Mary, to John's care, saying, *"Woman, here is your son"* (John 19:26), and to John, *"Here is your mother"* (verse 27). No greater honor was ever paid to a disciple than this touching assignment.

I feel that we have opened a rich treasure here in John's gospel. His relationship to the Trinity was one of unconditional and powerfully functional love, and he came to be known as "the beloved disciple." It is no surprise therefore that in his gospel we have a remarkable window into the inner working of this central paradigm of the relationship that characterizes the cosmos—the Father and the Son! And just as John closely observed and entered into the Father/Son paradigm, we can to do the same as we spread the Kingdom of God in the world.

The Fatherhood Vacuum

Everything we have discussed to this point is wonderful news for humankind, because the world today is suffering great turmoil due to a massive "Fatherhood vacuum" that has created a crisis of orphanhood—biological, emotional, and spiritual. An orphan is one who has uncertain affinity, who is parentless, fatherless, without a true family. In our culture, the family, which is the basic unit of a healthy and ordered society, finds itself in a heated battle for its very survival. An unprecedented spiritual attack is being mounted against everything that has to do with family, leading to many troubling symptoms. Fathers are absent from homes, with single mothers raising their children alone. For various reasons, many fathers are unable or unwilling to develop a strong relationship with their children and to mentor them. Added to these problems are issues of parental neglect, child abuse, and more. Children everywhere are suffering from a spirit of orphanhood, and this often stays with them in adulthood.

The church is not immune to this Fatherhood vacuum because many believers have experienced—and are experiencing—the same societal and familial conditions. Consequently, they have not understood their relationship to God the Father or accepted His heart of love for them. Most have also not had a spiritual mother or father in the church to love, affirm, and guide them. This is a serious issue because our view of God and the Kingdom will be woefully deficient until we truly see and experience God as Father.

John Arnott, the loveable spiritual giant who pastored the Toronto Airport Christian Fellowship through one of the greatest moves of God in recent history, stated in his foreword to a book on the Father's heart, "I believe with all my heart that the message of the Father's love is one of the most important messages to be shared in today's world." The stated motto of the "Toronto Blessing" was "Receiving the Father's Love and Giving it Away." A few years after the beginning of that powerful spiritual inferno, which began early in 1994, John planned and carried out a conference on the Kingdom of God, and I was invited to be one of the speakers. I feel that my contribution was meager because God had only begun to unfold to me the magnificent, magnetic mysteries of the Kingdom, but I came away from that conference with the conviction that the secret to the lasting power of the Toronto Blessing was its being linked to the Kingdom and its King-Father.

Today, over twenty years later, that conviction is not only still with me but is stronger than ever. The church where the Toronto Blessing started still burns brightly in a dozen expressions across the metropolis of Toronto. Furthermore, thousands of churches across the world bear the marks of transformation from the impact of that great move of God. Anything we are involved in must be Kingdom-centered, Kingdom-motivated, and Kingdom empowered, or what we are doing will come to nothing or less than nothing. The Kingdom of God is forever—its increase and peace will never cease. (See Isaiah 9:7 NKJV, KJV, ESV.) Thus, whatever happens in the church that is linked to the Kingdom will continue.

Recently, there was a revival in America in which hundreds of thousands of people gathered over some months to witness thousands of seekers come to Christ. While this was a wonderful result, I heard someone who was a part of that move say, "I am asked why this revival did not last. I can tell you why: it was never connected with the Kingdom of God." In other words, it was connected to the church and to the gospel of the atonement, but it wasn't connected to the fullness of the Kingdom, so it did not have a foundation to sustain it.

One of the quotes at the beginning this chapter was by Thomas Smail. His book, *The Forgotten Father*, was a caution to the charismatic movement that the greatest need of this movement was to prioritize seeking the Father—or be prepared for a downgrade in overall significance. "If I were to diagnose and prescribe for its present ills in a single sentence, I would say that it needs to know the Father," he wrote.[27] Smail's message was either not heard, or it was heard but not heeded. In my opinion, the movement's inattention to this message led to one of the greatest seasons of confusion, division, moral failure, and scandal in the history of the church worldwide. Smail's book deserves, even at this late date, a reading from us all.

---

27. Smail, *Forgotten Father*, 13.

The Cure for Orphanhood

There is a sure cure for orphanhood in its various forms in the church and in the world. The Father/Son paradigm, functioning between both spiritual and biological fathers and sons, is the operating system of the mighty Kingdom of God. The heavenly Father desires His redeemed children to join with Him in addressing the Fatherhood vacuum by helping to transform spiritual orphans into new Kingdom sons and daughters, and by translating the message of the Kingdom into living relationships that will make the world a better place, glorifying God and healing wounds, divisions, isolation, and loneliness.

> *Ask the Holy Spirit to release*
> *the Father's love into your heart.*

The first step we must take is to receive our adoption as God's child through faith in Christ, and accept His forgiveness. Second, many of us also need to receive a massive dose of the Father's love, prompted by the Spirit moving our orphan's spirit to cry, *"Abba* [Daddy], *Father!"* (Romans 8:15; Galatians 4:6). This is the work of the Spirit alone, and such an experience can be powerful enough to fully eradicate an orphan spirit. Follow-up is indispensable; and if the cure is carefully guarded, it will be inevitable and continuous. In this process, finding a trusted believer to be one's spiritual parent can also lead to and secure newfound healing and wholeness. Ask the Spirit to release the Father's love into your heart and into the hearts of those to whom you minister.

I came into a working knowledge of the Father/Son paradigm by spiritual instinct as I began to respond to an inner concern for younger preachers, a concern that I fully believe was the result of God sharing His own

Father's heart with me. A bit later, I began to discover that the relational structure of the Kingdom is family. It was at this point that I started to do intentionally what I had previously done instinctively.

Some years ago, I was asked by a spiritual leader what legacy I planned to leave. My immediate answer was, "Leave? I'm not going anywhere!" It wasn't long before I reconsidered the question, knowing that it was inevitable, if Jesus tarried, that I would leave this world. Subsequently, I felt that I needed to recognize and articulate the legacy God wanted me to bestow. Here is that legacy:

> I plan to leave sons who have sons who have sons who have sons, to the edge of eternity, who are *discovering* the Kingdom of God, *declaring* the Kingdom of God, and *demonstrating* the Kingdom of God until Jesus comes.

To my delight, this is happening across the world; reports are coming from sons around the globe who are living and ministering the Kingdom on earth! Missionary ventures, fueled with the Kingdom gospel and fired by the Father/Son paradigm, are seeing churches spring up that are veritable ignition points for signs and wonders of biblical proportion. The Father is sending sons, and sons are becoming fathers in increasing numbers, so that the additions of yesterday are becoming the multiplications of today and tomorrow.

Please understand that when I use the word "sons," I am referring to all true believers, male and female. As Paul instructed us:

> *For you are all sons of God through faith in Christ Jesus.*
> (Galatians 3:26)

> *But when the fullness of the time had come, God sent forth His Son, born of a woman, born under the law, to redeem those who were under the law, that we might receive the adoption as sons. And because you are sons, God has sent forth the Spirit of His Son into your hearts, crying out, "Abba, Father!" Therefore you are no longer a slave but a son, and if a son, then an heir of God through Christ.*
> (Galatians 4:4–7 NKJV)

My biological son, Tim, felt it was a part of his own spiritual call to yoke himself with me in this ministry of spiritual fathers and sons, especially for the purpose of stewarding the generational continuation of discovering, declaring, and demonstrating the Kingdom of God to every successive son until Jesus returns. My only hesitation was the fear that such a move might cloud his own personal call. His rapid reply to this fear was, "Dad, this *is* my legacy!"

Tim and I had always endeavored to model a proper and reproducible relationship as father and son. Throughout his life, Tim has sought to be a father-pleaser, in the best sense, as has my daughter, Tammy. To my indescribable pleasure, they have both succeeded! So Tim and I began our adventure into this stewardship of fatherhood and sonship, proceeding with purposefulness what we had been doing somewhat intuitively for years while teaching the perfect Father/Son model in the relationship between God the Father and Jesus the Son. And as a result of our continued fatherhood ministry, my greatest privilege, now that I am in my eighties, is being a spiritual father to several hundred sons and daughters across the world.[28]

When God moved powerfully in revival in the church I pastored a half-century ago, there was barely time to tell of a previous miracle of healing, deliverance, or spiritual restoration because a flood of other reports would crowd out the former ones with more recent and current Kingdom happenings. This seems to be what is occurring today with the recovery of the Kingdom message and mentality, including the Father/Son paradigm. One only has to lightly investigate to find that, across the world, God is moving with such lightening-like swiftness and such culture-changing power that it defies the imagination and baffles the understanding. God has always employed the family paradigm to advance His Kingdom on earth, and He has not changed!

In Leif Hetland's splendid foreword to this book, he recalls asking me what the Kingdom, operating through the church in the world, would look like in its full expression. My rather hesitating and incomplete answer, which I gave at the spur of the moment, was this: "Son, I do not know. All I know is that the Kingdom will only be entrusted through family." Though I now confess that this answer was the only thing that came to mind, I was,

---

28. See sonslink.com.

by the grace of God, spot-on. Today, several years older and hopefully a bit wiser, I am more prepared for the question! My answer is that the Kingdom is entrusted through family, but also, without this component, nothing else in the church will fully succeed as it was intended to by its Lord.

> *Jesus is coming for a family—*
>
> *not an organization or a religious system.*

For example, the fivefold ministry of the church, outlined by Paul in Ephesians 4:11, was surely not established without the foundation of the Father/Son paradigm. As vital as the fivefold component is, it is destined to fail without this pattern. It is my studied and somewhat stubborn opinion that unless pastors, teachers, apostles, prophets, and evangelists first become sons and fathers, their best efforts, regardless of their high intentions and their commitment, are doomed to lesser influence than God intended. The family component needs to be the church's main operating system—with every leader becoming a son first and then a father who trains, inspires, and imparts to the next generation of leaders.

The Spirit is moving in the hearts of all God's children to draw them to sonship, and through sonship to God the Father and fatherhood/mentorship. Jesus is coming for a family—not an organization or a religious system, but a living, breathing, organic family within the larger Kingdom of God!

The Parable of the Loving Father

As I wrote earlier, if the church is to recover the Kingdom, and if we are to be healed of the orphan spirit and bring healing to others, we must truly understand and receive the love of our heavenly Father. Therefore, to conclude this chapter, I want to try to communicate to you the depth of God's love for you through a familiar but powerful story.

In my opinion, the greatest story Jesus ever told is what is known as the parable of the prodigal son. (See Luke 15:11–32.) I actually prefer a different title, because its common name is clearly a mistake. I think that the chapter headings in various Bibles—which are not part of the inspired text but were added later—sometimes seem to miss the main point of the passage. In this parable, neither the younger brother nor the older brother is the main actor. They are, simply put, bit players in a much larger story. The famed parable is really about a persistently loving and forgiving father. (Similarly, the story of the lost coin is about a responsible, thoughtful housekeeper; and the story of the lost sheep concerns a faithful, thoughtful shepherd.)

The Younger Son's Decision

Allow me to paraphrase this parable. An estate owner has two sons. The younger son is restless and cannot bear to stay home under his father's care. He is determined to explore the world; therefore, he makes a request of his father that is legal, though ill-advised—he wants to receive his inheritance early to do what he wants with it now. The father grants his son's request, though he probably knows it will not be in his son's best interests. (Fathers often do that. They give a wayward son what he wants and withhold what he really needs.) So, not many days later, the younger son, caving in to his ignorance, gathers up his inheritance and leaves his father's home.

It's not clear how much time passes between the stages of this story, but we can imagine that things happened rather quickly. The younger son's dreams of women, wine, and song soon turn into a nightmare. In a short while, he has squandered his entire inheritance, and he ends up as a slop-dealer on a hog farm, so hungry he could eat the fare of pigs. And what do you know? The young man "comes to his senses." Here is his reasoning:

How many of my father's hired hands have more than enough food, and here I am dying of hunger! I'll get up, go to my father, and say to him, Father, I have sinned against heaven and in your sight. I'm no longer worthy to be called your son. Make me like one of your hired hands. (Luke 15:17–19)

The son immediately acts on his decision. He gets up and heads home.

The Father's Response

Now, let's change scenes and return to the father's house. Remember that this powerful story is about the father. You will not get the point of the parable until you really understand that. The father is where he has gone every day of his son's absence—sitting, standing, or pacing on the porch of the family mansion as he wishes, hopes, and prays for his youngest boy's return. On this day, he shades his eyes against the sun and catches the sight of something moving in the distance. He rubs his eyes and shakes his head to clear his mind, and his heart accelerates as recognition dawns—"It's my son! It's my boy coming home!"

And then his legs get the message. The father flies on wings of love to meet the returning wretch. Listen to the description of the moving reunion: *"But while the son was still a long way off, his father saw him and was filled with compassion. He ran, threw his arms around his neck, and kissed him"* (Luke 15:20). Never mind the sight of the bedraggled creature his son has become. Never mind the putrid smell of the hog pen. Never mind anything—he has gotten his boy back!

Now that the son is home, we can pause to ask a pressing question. Since he has already used up his inheritance, what will be his relationship to the family and to the estate in its present operations, as well as in its future plans? Only the father can answer this question. Only he can decide. Thus, the pivotal component in this story is the father's response.

What happens next? I think that the son, weeping as he must have been, gently pushes his father away, clears his throat, and begins his rehearsed speech, saying, *"I have sinned.... I'm no longer worthy to be called your son"* (Luke 15:21). But he never gets to finish the rest of this carefully-crafted speech. His father interrupts him before he can utter the last part, *"Make me like one of your hired hands"* (Luke 15:19). Turning toward the big house, where, by now, the whole crowd of servants are witnesses to the novel scene, the father cries out,

> *"Quick! Bring out the best robe and put it on him; put a ring on his finger and sandals on his feet. Then bring the fattened calf and slaughter it, and let's celebrate with a feast, because this son of mine was dead and is alive again; he was lost and is found!" So, they began to celebrate.*
>
> (Luke 15:22–24)

Do you feel it? The whole culture of the place has changed. Everyone on this working estate, with all its demands, procedures, and chores, interrupts their activities and suddenly begins a joyful, long-awaited celebration that is heard by the entire neighboring countryside.

The Father's response, revealed in his instructions to his servants, was direct and unambiguous: "Bring the best robe, a ring for his finger, and shoes for his feet. Kill the fatted calf, and let's celebrate!" What does he mean this? Which robe, what ring, what calf? In each case, it is the one the father has set aside for the son whose repentance and return he had not only prayed for and believed in but had also waited for and expected. The father was not surprised! He had been well-prepared.

In his splendid book *Sonship: The Word Made Flesh*, Jim McNally observes wisely that the son came to self-realization in the pigpen but not necessarily repentance.[29] This warning has led me to the solemn conclusion that true repentance alone will bring us to full reconciliation with our heavenly Father. We might therefore ask, "Hasn't the grieved soul of the father overridden good, common sense and caused him to forget what the son did in forsaking him and going his own way?"

Follow carefully the next statements, because otherwise you might miss the point: we have no right or reason to press the issue of the son's repentance until we put the spotlight on the father and focus on the power and potential of father-love. Perhaps (even probably), the son's repentance was far from complete. But when we consider what the son expressed about his need to change, the situation becomes explosive with revelation. When

---

29. See McNally, *Sonship*, 27–29.

he came to himself, he said, in effect, "My dad's hired hands have all they need to eat, and here I am starving to death."

These words don't necessarily indicate a repentant heart. But the son has begun the kind of thinking that, if properly followed through, can lead to genuine repentance: *"I'll get up, go to my father, and say to him, Father, I have sinned against heaven and in your sight. I'm no longer worthy to be called your son. Make me like one of your hired hands"* (Luke 15:18–19).

> *It is the Father's love that brings forth the true fruit of contrition.*

As a first step toward true repentance before God, self-realization must be followed by steps of self-disclosure and bowing in humility and total commitment to the will of the Father. This is the point toward which I have been moving. Though the son may not yet have fully repented, his reasoning had led him to the right place where he *could* experience repentance—the presence of his loving father. We need to remember that it is the goodness of God that leads us to repentance (see Romans 2:4); it is the Father's love that brings forth the true fruit of contrition. In the blessed shadow of the Father's love, true and full repentance is given a path in which to walk.

If there is a prodigal reading these words right now, I remind you that you have a heavenly Father waiting for you with the robe of righteousness, the ring of sonship, and the sandals of His future plans for you. These things are yours and await your return to Him. The fattened calf will soon become your feast. Let's celebrate your return! It's all about the Father!

But wait for the rest of the story.

This Second Prodigal Stayed Home

The main part of the story is complete. The departed son is home, washed outside and in. The party has begun! But there is a fly in the ointment, a frog in the soup, a weed in the garden (and there generally is). The elder brother comes in from the field, hears the sounds of music and merriment, and inquires of a servant, "What's going on?" The answer causes him to have a sudden fit of anger that reveals the heart of a Pharisee, as well as the heart of an orphan: "Your brother is back, and your dad has thrown a party!"

What happens next? *"He became angry and didn't want to go in"* (Luke 15:28).

The father is informed of this development and leaves the party to calm the affronted son, who greets his father with a hail of bitterness and a blast of stinging words:

> *Look, I have been slaving many years for you, and I have never disobeyed your orders, yet you never gave me a young goat so I could celebrate with my friends. But when this son of yours came, who had devoured your assets with prostitutes, you slaughtered the fattened calf for him.* (Luke 15:29–30)

To these words we might add the growl of a mad dog or the hissing of an offended cat! It turns out that the older son was, at heart, not much better than his younger brother, Mr. Dumb and Selfish. He was fighting mad over the good news of his younger brother's homecoming and the ensuing party, so he broke into a cussin' fit. But remember, neither brother is what it is all about. Let's hear it for—that's right—good old Dad, the only cool dude on the ranch.

Now, read my lips, "It's all about the Father!"

Examine the older brother's statement for a moment, which is sadly adorned with *"I," "me,"* and *"my."* Accusation against his father follows quickly after self-justification: *"You never...."* But enough about the offended brother. Listen carefully to the brief entreaty of the father:

> *"Son," he said to him, "you are always with me, and everything I have is*
> *yours. But we had to celebrate and rejoice, because this brother of yours*
> *was dead and is alive again; he was lost and is found."*
>
> (Luke 15:31–32)

This story, with all its complexities, ends rather abruptly with the above statements. It seems unlike Jesus to end a story without a finish. I am not often one to leave a mystery alone without a question, so I asked God if there was a good reason for this. I try to be discerning about attributing to God thoughts and ideas that come to me, but sometimes (more often than not) I get an answer that is so clearly from heaven that I cannot doubt it. The following is the summation of what I heard: "This is a story that calls for an answer from every offended person. Will you lay aside your offense in favor of the Father's reassuring love and make a contribution to the family party God desires for us all, or will you treasure your offense as something more valuable than what's going on with the family of God? You will write the conclusion to the story!"

I firmly believe that if Jesus had finished the parable, it would have described the overpowering love of the Father healing the elder brother of his offense and of his pharisaism. Here's the way I think the story would have ended. The father and his older son stand in the fading light of the setting sun. The son has emptied his heart of bitterness, accusation, and isolation. He is fuming, his face is set, and his hands are hanging at his sides, curled into fists. The father reaches out and places a hand on each shoulder, as any real, loving father would want to do. The father's words escape his lips as softly as a falling rose petal as he says:

"Son,...you are always with me"—the feature of the father's abiding presence.

"...everything I have is yours"—the fact of the father's abundant provision.

"...this brother of yours was dead and is alive again; he was lost and is found"—the force of the father's accomplished purpose.

The gentle words of the father have landed softly in the heart of the son. A full moment passes, seeming like eternity. Under the father's hands, the shoulders of the son begin to relax, and a sigh slowly escapes from his lips. His chin begins to drop toward his chest as tears race from under his closed eyelids downward into his grimy beard. Then he says, his voice almost a whisper, with a softness much like his father's, "Dad, I'm so sorry. I love my brother, and I'm glad he's home. Tell him I will join the celebration as soon as I clean myself up and properly dress."

The father goes back to the scene of the celebration, beckons his younger son, relays what the older brother has just said, and, with a satisfied smile, returns to the joyous crowd. In a few minutes, the doors swing open to the party room, and there stands the older brother. He stops for a moment as the crowd, noticing his presence, grows silent. Finally, his gaze meets that of...his brother. After a few seconds' pause, the two race to the center of the room to be lost in each other's arms, melting every offence and bridging the long distance between them. And the happy father makes it three! The father's love has won again, and the party takes on new life!

I honestly believe that's how it would have ended, and I pray that's how it ends now with you. It's all about the Father!

The Return of the Prodigals

Before time began, God was Father. His creative acts were the acts of a Father. He has not changed the trajectory of His original plan to populate the universe with His very own family ruling at His side. Even now, I am reaching for a higher understanding, a clearer revelation, of these astounding truths.

> I'd part with all the joys of sense
> To gaze upon thy throne;
> Pleasures spring fresh for ever thence,
> Unspeakable, unknown.[30]

---

30. Isaac Watts, 1709.

The Father/Son paradigm of the Kingdom is not just a theological axiom that is important for us to know to have correct doctrine. We must have a revelation of the identity of God as our Father, a life-centering event in which the Holy Spirit within us cries, *"Abba, Father!"* (Romans 8:15; Galatians 4:6). This will lead to a relationship with the Father as His child that is a continuous lifestyle, a relationship of loving commitment and faithful obedience.

The world is waiting with great expectation to witness the manifestation of the sons of God. (See Romans 8:19.) This expectation will come to pass only when the Father is revealed through His spiritual sons and daughters. Jesus the Son revealed God the Father to the world; and the church, indwelt by the Son, must renew its understanding of the Father and its close relationship with Him, so it can demonstrate His everlasting love to all people. Then the church will help to restore the family of the earth to God. The prodigals are coming home!

13

KINGDOM SPOTLIGHT ON THE CHILDREN

L et me begin this chapter with a caution: Don't underestimate the value of children!

Brandon Donnell is a mild-mannered, humble, soft-spoken, and deeply spiritual missionary who has a children's home in Kenya, Africa. In a recent sons' event in Texas in which Brandon became a spiritual son, he was moved to share with the group his experience in which God revealed His own heart for children. The result was a vision for a million children rescued from hopeless orphanhood, loved, led to Jesus, filled with the Spirit, discipled in Kingdom power, and released to win Africa to Jesus.

Brandon reported, "I believe I get a new angel every time I take in another abandoned child. Jesus said, '*Most assuredly, I say to you, hereafter you shall see heaven open, and the angels of God ascending and descending upon the Son of Man.*' The angels are assigned to protect the children." (See John 1:51 NKJV; Matthew 18:10.)

Not only did Brandon capture all our hearts for the children, but I became convinced I could not write a book on the Kingdom without putting a spotlight on the children of the world. For this reason, and because of the light that has been shed in my own heart regarding the Kingdom and children, I must urge you to remember the children in the coming days as the gospel of the Kingdom sweeps like a prairie fire across the world.

Undervaluing Children

The Father/Son paradigm of the Kingdom requires us to seriously re-think our current attitudes and actions toward children. This is because a Kingdom outlook is antithetical to the fallen mind-set and the way it approaches relationships. While some positive and helpful views of children are being promoted in our world, many erroneous ones are also being advocated and practiced. And while there are many loving parents who model the Father's heart, I believe the following appraisal reflects widespread flawed attitudes toward children in our world. Although these issues are complex and cannot be fully discussed here, they do point to overall perspectives that are deficient and harmful.

> *To assess the values of any nation,*
> *one need only witness how it treats its children.*

It has been said that in order to assess the values of any nation, one need only witness how it treats its children. And it seems as if every nation or culture has practices, customs, rules of behavior, and assumptions that clearly demonstrate their failure to comprehend children's true worth. For the most part, children are perceived as little adults waiting to come of age, and whose value is minimal until that time. In the meanwhile, they are tolerated more than celebrated. Little children may be thought of as cute and cuddly, but they are also considered to be costly and inconvenient, though that inconvenience is generally perceived to be worth the price of raising them to adulthood. Some parents, rather than consider their children an inconvenience, tend to overindulge and cater to them, unintentionally showing them a lack of respect and much-needed discipline.

In many nations, children are valued chiefly for their potential contributions to family productivity and boosting the nation's economy; thus, large families are encouraged and rewarded. Other countries, citing overcrowding, have legally limited the number of children a family can have. On the whole, it is safe to say that all nations, including the United States, have fallen far short of seeing children through heaven's eyes, and endorsing and upholding their essential value in the culture.

The Abuse of Children

Evidence of the failure to value children is apparent in many ways, some of them terrifying. Because of the supposition of their lack of importance, children are being greatly abused. In general, they are the most unprotected people group in the world, mainly because they are unable to defend themselves against the whims of parents, other relatives, communities, and cultural demands. Historically, one of the most frightening abuses of children, practiced by some ancient cultures and religions, was the human sacrifice of babies and children to appease the gods. Today, one of the worst forms of violence against children is abortion, with some nations using overpopulation or the "uselessness" of children as their justification for the practice. Yet whether or not the practice is supported by law, and regardless of whether it is celebrated as a civil right or used as a religious ritual, abortion is the tragic *taking of a human life*. It is murder. Again, the ultimate issue behind abortion is a lack of perceived value in unborn children. Other terrible violations against children take the form of physical, emotional, or sexual abuse.

Discovering Our Greatest Treasure

The bottom line with this issue of the devaluation of children and their place in humankind—and particularly in the Kingdom of God—is that *"all have sinned and fall[en] short of the glory of God"* (Romans 3:23) in neglecting to see children as full human beings with rich possibilities and phenomenal gifts of high present value to the God who created the universe. We must recognize the wholesale failure of every nation and culture on the planet to assess the worth and potential power of the children among us.

Such discounting of children is an ideal place for the church to begin its repentance as we prepare to restore the Kingdom on earth. If we can see just a hint of the true worth of babies—those who are yet to be born, as well as newborns—toddlers, children, and young people, we just may be awakened to the greatest Kingdom treasure on the earth. Let's hear it for the kids!

Valuing Our Children

Do you think I have perhaps gone too far in putting the Kingdom spotlight on our children? If I have, then I am in wonderful company, because this is exactly what Jesus did as *"the way, the truth and the life,"* without whom no one can come to the Father. (See John 14:6.) His teachings can establish in our minds and hearts the same vital assessment of worth for children that the Father has for them

In the accounts of Jesus' ministry in the Gospels, He often seems to qualify as the Prince of the Unexpected—either by *saying* something completely out of people's frame of reference or by *doing* something that totally blows the minds of those watching Him. The following biblical account, which centers on children, includes both of these expressions, each strengthening the case for the other. The story commences in this way:

> At that time the disciples came to Jesus and said, "Who is greatest is the Kingdom of heaven?"   (Matthew 18:1)

It is likely that the disciples had just been having a discussion among themselves about which of them was the greatest in the Kingdom. (See Luke 9:46–48.) None of them was prepared for Jesus' reply to their question. Well, He did not really reply at first, but He did respond. He called a child and stood him in their midst. Then He communicated some rather shocking truths:

> "I assure you," He said, "unless you are converted and become like children, you will never enter the kingdom of heaven. Therefore, whoever humbles himself like this child—this one is the greatest in the kingdom of heaven." (Matthew18:3–4)

In the next two verses, Jesus provided some additional significant information about children:

> And whoever welcomes one child like this in My name welcomes Me. But whoever causes the downfall of one of these little ones who believe in Me—it would be better for him if a heavy millstone were hung around his neck and he were drowned in the depths of the sea! (Matthew 18:5–6)

Wow! Jesus is serious about the matter of children! Our Kingdom journey requires that we give close attention to what He is saying. It seems as if, in answering the disciples' question about greatness, Jesus is issuing a major warning about not overlooking, underrating, or violating any child. It gets more serious; read on.

> See that you don't look down on one of these little ones, because I tell you that in heaven their angels continually view the face of My Father in heaven. (Matthew 18:10)

Do you see what I see here? Let's not pass over these statements too lightly. Jesus is discussing Kingdom principles, and He places children directly in the middle of the discussion.

Permit me to go back and summarize the scene between Jesus and His disciples. It all starts with a question about who is greatest in the Kingdom of God. Jesus seizes upon the question and calls a little child to His side to inform His listeners that the Kingdom is closed to anybody who does not become like that child. It's almost as if the question about greatness had touched a sensitive nerve in Him, so that He goes into "furthermore" mode. You can almost feel the heat of His rhetoric where He says, in effect,

"And I will tell you another thing while I am on this point, you adults are just obsolete children, and you're going to have to humble yourself and become like this child in order to even enter the Kingdom, let alone be the greatest in it!" Then, even more seriously, He says, "If you offend one of these little ones, you'd be better off strapped to a big rock and thrown into the ocean!" Finally, He gives perhaps the most frightening warning of all: "You're being watched from heaven. These kids each have an angel who continually views the face of the Father."

> *The Kingdom is open only to those*
> *who become like children, humbling themselves.*

What is He saying? Evidently, at birth, each child is assigned an angel from God's throne who is responsible for overseeing and caring for them. One sin against the child—even being dismissive toward, undervaluing, neglecting, offending, or overlooking them—is carefully noted in heaven. The child will have justice, and the offender punished. This may occur either immediately, at some point during the child's earthly life, or when God brings judgment at the end of time, unless the offender has truly repented.

Bottom line: Children are vital to God's world. Don't mess with the kids, or you're in big trouble!

Next, let us read another account involving Jesus and His disciples, which happened not long after the disciples asked their question about greatness in the Kingdom:

> *Then children were brought to [Jesus] so He might put His hands on them and pray. But the disciples rebuked them. Then Jesus said, "Leave the children alone, and don't try to keep them from coming to Me, because the Kingdom of heaven is made up of people like this."*
>
> (Matthew 19:13–14)

Other Bible versions translate the end of verse 14 as, *"…of such is the Kingdom of heaven"* (NKJV, KJV). I am deeply touched by this phrase, more so than at any other time in my life. To whom did Jesus refer when He used the description *"such"*? Obviously, in context, He was referring primarily to the children on earth in His day. They mattered greatly to Him. He had time for them, and He spent time with them. To Jesus, children were not a side issue; He did not consider them less than complete, valuable people. He deeply loved them and, as we have seen, He let it be known in clear terms that to abuse, offend, or even discount or overlook them is a serious breach of spiritual protocol. As Jesus said in the parable of the faithful Shepherd, *"It is not the will of your Father in heaven that one of these little ones perish"* (Matthew 18:14).

Beyond the immediate context, however, I think that *"such"* refers to children of all times, including today. Some of these children have come of age and become purposeful followers of Jesus. But the reference surely includes millions of children who have not yet come to the age of accountability and who are covered by God's grace. There is a theological term for this, called "prevenient grace."

Additionally, the term would include all children who have either died in the womb (due to physical complications or abortion), were stricken by disease, or were killed by other means. Where are all these little ones? Renowned preacher Charles Haddon Spurgeon wrote:

> When I think of all the multitudes of babies who have died, who now are swarming in the streets of Heaven, it does seem to me to be a blessed thought that albeit generation after generation of adults have passed away in unbelief and rebellion, yet enormous multitudes of children have gone streaming up to Heaven, saved by the Grace of God, through the death of Christ, to sing the high praises of the Lord forever before the Eternal Throne! "Of such is the kingdom of Heaven." They give tone and character to the kingdom! It is rather a kingdom of children than of men.[31]

---

31. Charles Spurgeon, "Receiving the Kingdom of God as a Little Child," sermon, October 20, 1878, Metropolitan Tabernacle, Newington, England, http://www.ccel.org/ccel/spurgeon/sermons24.xlix.html.

Billions of children are in heaven right now, praising God. Multiplied millions of children on earth are joining in, and they, along with millions of "adult children," will comprise an end-time army of worshipping warriors in God's Kingdom, armed with the weapons of unconditional love, praise, and the gospel of the Kingdom, initiating mass cultural transformation.

"A Kingdom of Children"

Thus, we must recognize that children are essential to God's eternal Kingdom and purposes. It is said that every newborn baby is a certificate of declaration that God has not lost confidence in the human race. None of us can ignore the slightest tolerance in us to fail to value the place that God has given children in His Kingdom. Perhaps no higher affirmation ever escaped the lips of Jesus than in these two declarations:

> *Unless you are converted and become like children, you will never enter the Kingdom of heaven.* (Matthew 18:3)

> *Leave the children alone, and don't try to keep them from coming to Me, because the Kingdom of heaven is made up of people [such] like this.* (Matthew 19:14)

I have repeated these verses because they deserve our full attention. As I have shined the Kingdom spotlight on the issue of children, I have been stricken with the idea that we really must place ourselves alongside the children among the Kingdom throng, or we will be "missing in action" in the expansion of God's Kingdom on earth. Entering the Kingdom is out of the question without a childlike spirit. Notice I didn't say "childish" spirit. To walk in the Kingdom is to walk in childlike innocence, transparency, and sincerity, as we discussed in chapter 9, "Seek First the Kingdom: Life's Most Important Adventure."

We adults must remember this: our significance and identity are not to be found in what we have accomplished, how well we are known, or how much of the world's wealth we have amassed. Our essential identity is to be found in our relationship to God as His children, living in His love. Let us voice the refrain,

> Gentle Jesus, meek and mild,
> Look upon a little child;
> Pity my simplicity,
> Suffer me to come to Thee.[32]

Yes, there is only one way to come to Jesus and the Kingdom: the child's way! Shepherd or sage, philosopher or peasant, high or low, let us all come to Jesus as adoring children and go out to the world as excited children to spread the gospel of His Kingdom. The light of the Kingdom is shining on you and me, while ringing in our ears is the single qualifying factor for Kingdom life:

> *Unless you are converted and become like children, you will never enter the Kingdom of heaven.*   (Matthew 18:3)

I love the little song that many of us have sung all our lives:

Jesus loves the little children
All the children of the world.
Red and yellow, black and white,
They are precious in His sight.
Jesus loves the little children of the world.

I especially like the "revised" version:

Jesus loves the little children,
All the children of the world.
Every color, every race,
They are covered by His grace.
Jesus loves the little children of the world.[33]

---

32. Charles Wesley, "Gentle Jesus, Meek and Mild," 1742, http://www.hymntime.com/tch/htm/g/e/n/gentleje.htm.

33. C. H. Woolston, "Jesus Loves the Little Children," *The Baptist Hymnal*, Convention Press (Nashville: Broadman Press 1991), word alt. copyright 1991 Broadman Press, http://www.hymnary.org/text/jesus_loves_the_little_children_all_the.

Let us pray, "Father, make me like a child again!" May we follow in the footsteps of our Father-King and love all children while seeking to be like them in our Kingdom entrance and our Kingdom walk!

14

HOW THE KINGDOM CAME; HOW THE KINGDOM COMES

God's reign over the entire cosmos is eternal; it has always existed and will forever exist. The rule of His Kingdom on earth is a plan that He originated and orchestrated. He desired that a perfect government direct our world, and being sovereign, it is a purpose that He will fully complete. Jesus coming into this world was the initiation of His restoration plan to reestablish His Kingdom among humanity.

When God enacts an enterprise, He does so not only successfully, but exactingly. We can therefore expect that the ways in which the Kingdom was restored through Jesus provide us with secrets to how it can be best facilitated and expanded on earth now and in the future. By studying and applying these ways, we can cooperate with God in the continuation—and culmination—of His purposes. Hence the title, "How the Kingdom Came; How the Kingdom Comes."

This chapter naturally divides itself into two parts: (1) The protocol for how the Kingdom was recovered on earth through Christ after the fall of humanity—mainly focusing on the ways God worked through human beings to further His purposes, and their necessary response. (2) The protocol for how the Kingdom will be reintroduced on earth to spread the message and mentality of the Kingdom gospel. God's primary method of working through His people has not changed. Thus, it matters much what we do with the now! As the old adage says, "The past is history; the future is mystery; now is a gift; that's the reason we call it the present."

How the Kingdom Came

God Used Key Earthly Players (with Some Angelic Help)

When God the Father restored the Kingdom to earth through Jesus Christ, He moved in the lives of various people to help usher it in. Here is a list of cast members in the cosmic event of the birth of Jesus Christ—the drama of the ages—each one playing a part that was indispensable to the whole plan of God:

Zechariah: A temple priest of Abijah's division who was on duty when the drama surfaced.

Elizabeth: The wife of Zechariah, who was descended from Aaron.

Gabriel: The angel that God sent to Zechariah, Mary, and Joseph.

Mary: A teenage girl, engaged to be married to Joseph, who will become the mother of Jesus.

Joseph: The righteous man to whom Mary is engaged.

Simeon: A righteous and devout man to whom the Holy Spirit gave the assurance he would not die before he saw the Lord's Messiah.

Anna: A prophetess who is over a hundred years old and has been a widow for eighty-four years.

Now let us look at the stories of these players in a little more detail, describing their unique participation in the restoration of God's Kingdom on earth.

Zechariah and Elizabeth

Zechariah and Elizabeth were a devout but childless couple who are described in Scripture in this way:

Both were righteous in God's sight, living without blame according to all the commands and requirements of the Lord. But they had no children because Elizabeth could not conceive, and both of them were well along in years.   (Luke 1:6–7)

As a priest in Israel, Zechariah was carrying out his duties in the Holy Place at the temple at Jerusalem when the angel Gabriel appeared to him with an astonishing promise from God: the Lord had heard his prayers for a child, and Zechariah and Elizabeth were about to become parents. They would have a son who would be named John. This son would awaken the people of Israel so they would be prepared for coming of the Messiah. (See Luke 1:8–17.)

At first, Zechariah stumbled in his belief, unable to take in the magnitude of this message.

"How can I know this?" Zechariah asked the angel. "For I am an old man, and my wife is well along in years." The angel answered him, "I am Gabriel, who stands in the presence of God, and I was sent to speak to you and tell you this good news. Now listen! You will become silent and unable to speak until the day these things take place, because you did not believe my words, which will be fulfilled in their proper time."
                                             (Luke 1:18–20)

Because her husband was mute, Elizabeth probably did not learn the whole story of the mysterious meeting between Zechariah and the angel Gabriel until sometime later. But I will leave it to you to imagine what went on in their household after he returned from this encounter. Discerning readers will get the point. A hint will suffice: it took mutual faith and God's grace to bring about what happened! When Elizabeth became pregnant, she expressed her faith in this way:

The Lord has done this for me. He has looked with favor in these days to take away my disgrace among the people.   (Luke 1:25)

We can see that Zechariah came to fully accept God's words through Gabriel, and that he and Elizabeth were unified in doing God's will, when their son was born, and they named him "John," as the angel had directed.

Now the time had come for Elizabeth to give birth, and she had a son. Then her neighbors and relatives heard that the Lord had shown her His great mercy, and they rejoiced with her. When they came to circumcise the child on the eighth day, they were going to name him Zechariah, after his father. But his mother responded, "No! He will be called John." Then they said to her, "None of your relatives has that name." So they motioned to his father to find out what he wanted him to be called. He asked for a writing tablet and wrote: HIS NAME IS JOHN. *And they were all amazed. Immediately his mouth was opened and his tongue set free, and he began to speak, praising God.*

(Luke 1:57–64)

After Zechariah's faith affirmation, he recovered his voice. The bottom line is that, against all custom and all probabilities, he believed the Lord and acted in accordance with God's word—his old age and Elizabeth's notwithstanding. What he had heard from God through the angel Gabriel came to pass. Hold this truth close as we continue.

Joseph

Let us not overlook Joseph's importance and his own necessary response of faith to the overwhelming circumstances surrounding the birth of Jesus. First, his betrothed, Mary, was found to be with child during their engagement period. There is no way to convey the shock that her pregnancy would have produced. According to Jewish custom, an engagement was the legal equivalent to a marriage. And according to the law, Joseph could have exposed Mary publicly for infidelity and ended the whole apparently sordid episode, going on with his life with his dignity intact. But the Scriptures say he was a *"righteous man"* (Matthew 1:19); he chose the high road and planned to divorce her quietly to prevent her from suffering public disgrace. However, an angelic visit changed these plans:

But after he had considered these things, an angel of the Lord suddenly appeared to him in a dream, saying, "Joseph, son of David, don't be afraid to take Mary as your wife, because what has been conceived in her is by the Holy Spirit. She will give birth to a son, and you are to

name Him Jesus, because He will save His people from their sins."
(Matthew 1:20–21)

Against all natural reason, Joseph joined the Kingdom narrative by believing the angel and receiving Mary, his betrothed who was with child by the Holy Spirit, as his wife. In obeying God, he became the silent hero and the stepfather of the Son of God! As Jesus' earthly father, Joseph's relationship with his Son was surely one of responsible mystery.

The Angel Gabriel

Gabriel and God's other angels on assignment in this cosmic drama manifested the supernatural component of His Kingdom plans. And angels are still important messengers and warriors today in carrying out His Kingdom purposes.

Gabriel not only visited Zechariah and Mary with messages from the Lord, but he is also likely the angel who appeared to Joseph in the dream to give him the "all clear" to wed Mary, informing him that the pregnancy was *"by the Holy Spirit"* (Matthew 1:20). Additionally, the day of Jesus' birth, an angel of the Lord, perhaps Gabriel again, appeared with a bright, heavenly light to shepherds in a field, terrifying them. But the angel informed them,

> *Don't be afraid, for look, I proclaim to you good news of great joy that will be for all the people: today a Savior, who is Messiah [Christ] the Lord, was born for you in the city of David. This will be sign for you: you will find a baby wrapped snugly in cloth and lying in a feeding trough [manger].* (Luke 2:10–12)

Suddenly, this single angel, having just announced the most transformational event in the history of the world, was joined by a huge choir of angels, making, I imagine, a thunderous sound as they sang.

> *Suddenly there was a multitude of the heavenly host with the angel, praising God and saying: "Glory to God in the highest heaven, and peace on earth to people He favors!"* (Luke 2:13–14)

An angel later warned Joseph to flee to Egypt with Mary and Jesus in order to escape King Herod of Palestine, who wanted to kill the child Jesus out of jealousy and fear of losing his earthly rule. An angel appeared to Joseph yet again after Herod died, with instructions to return to the land of Israel. (See Matthew 2.)

Simeon

When Mary and Joseph brought the baby Jesus to the temple to be dedicated, Simeon, a righteous and devout man guided by the Spirit, was there waiting for them. (See Luke 2:25–27.) He discerned that the baby was the One whom he had prophetically expected for a long time. Taking Jesus in his arms, he burst into this utterance of praise:

> *Lord, now You are letting your servant depart in peace, according to Your word; for my eyes have seen Your salvation that You have prepared in the presence of all peoples, a light for revelation to the Gentiles, and for glory to Your people Israel.* (Luke 2:29–32 ESV)

Anna

Anna, an elderly prophetess and longtime widow, was always in the temple complex day and night, fasting and praying. The Holy Spirit confirmed to her spirit, also, that the infant Jesus was the Messiah, and she joined Simeon in acknowledging who He was. (See Luke 1:36–38.) *"At that very moment, she came up and began to thank God and to speak about [Jesus] to all who were looking forward to the redemption of Jerusalem"* (Luke 2:38).

Thus, the above is a brief synopsis of the opening movement in the restoration of the Kingdom on earth, and the main players whom God used to bring it about. Heaven entered our world as God became man in the person of Jesus Christ. A virgin impregnated by a seed borne by the Spirit of the living God gave birth to the Son of God. God coming to earth as a human being is what is known as the *incarnation*, the greatest gift ever granted in the history of the planet, all wrapped up in love, mystery, tragedy, and triumph.

A significant event? So significant that it caused the entire fate of human beings to be altered, providing a way for them to be restored to their loving Creator. Eventually, it even led to a revision of our whole way of marking time, with our calendar based on the date that approximates the birth of Jesus Christ. What happened over two thousand years ago on planet Earth was such a vital event that we are reminded of it every time we look at a calendar, sign a contract, write a check, or compose a letter. Hence, when we use the term BC ("before Christ") or AD (*anno Domini*, "the year of our Lord"), we are acknowledging the justified fame of Jesus the Christ.

> *God coming to earth as a human being was the greatest gift ever granted in the history of the world.*

Is it not ironic that two thousand years after Jesus Christ lived on earth, we take for granted that this is the way we should measure time? What really happened in that era never dawns on most of the people who use this calendar system. I am actually surprised that there has not been an uprising to revise it. I expect it at any time. With the growth of other religions in the world, the God we worship, the Christ we follow, and the Holy Spirit whose Word we read and hear are becoming more and more contested in all cultures, even, or perhaps especially, in our own Western culture. There has been a trend to replace BC and AD with BCE ("before the Common Era") and CE ("Common Era"), but even this form is still based on the year of Christ's birth. I firmly believe that this dating system stands as a symbol of the existence of the eternal God who rules over an eternal Kingdom. But, I might add, if the present governments of this world should slowly or even suddenly undermine or outlaw this system of measuring time, it would not matter one bit to God's Kingdom plans or to our faith in Him as followers of Jesus.

Joining the Kingdom Narrative

Above, we reviewed significant events surrounding the birth of Jesus from the records found in the books of Luke and Matthew, but let me ask you a question: have you read the whole story lately—I mean the *whole* account as recorded in the gospels—as if you had never read it before? Then do so, right now! Then come back to this chapter.

Now honestly, have you ever read anything so downright outlandish, so outrageous, so unbelievable, and so offensive to your intellect as this story? Try to retell it as if you were giving an eyewitness report to a friend, speaking of angels, dreams, supernatural pregnancy out of wedlock, and an elderly husband and wife becoming parents when they were old enough to be grandparents—and then some. Then throw into the mix a gigantic angelic choir appearing out of thin air to shepherds who were caught in knee-knocking terror.

If you can tell this story with a straight face, without your audience walking out on you in irritated, agitated unbelief, I will be speechless. Talk about offending one's intelligence—this takes the cake! Perhaps, just perhaps, if we don't ever get this reaction, we have never really told the story, at least not in its unvarnished, unedited irony. On the other hand, it might be that we have told it so carefully that we have diluted it beyond offense. Maybe we have been too soft in the presentation or too weak in the application.

This dramatic story cannot just be told and left at that! It is simply too outlandish, too outrageous, to be presented without some explanation or reply to the inevitable question, "What does it all mean?" If the telling of this story does not stir up this question in us and in others, then it has either not been told accurately or it has not been heard properly. That is why (perhaps in stumbling fits and starts), I have sought to present this complex story as clearly as possible and with the purpose of leading us to discover the answer to this question. We can do this by taking a closer look at the players involved in the restoration of the Kingdom and what their response to God's call means for us today. So let's explore the observations that flow out of those first days of the Kingdom invasion. We will then seek to discover from the greatest story ever told how the story can be successfully carried on during these challenging and chaotic days in century twenty-one.

Each of the players in this cosmic drama made a choice to participate in the narrative of ushering in the Kingdom on earth. They each were asked by God, in essence, "Are you in this with Me?" and each responded, "I'm in!"

Zechariah recovered his good sense after his temporary stumble, standing as a model of faithful obedience in the midst of threatening social and religious circumstances. Even before his voice was restored by God and he prophesied (see Luke 1:67–79), his actions indicated that he was essentially praying to the Lord in his heart, "I am in!"

When Elizabeth became pregnant following the word from God to Zechariah, she surely realized that she was part of a much larger narrative. Against many odds, she accepted with joy this unlikely pregnancy in her old age and gave birth to John the Baptist, who prepared the way for the Messiah. Thus, she demonstrated her own faith in God's word, signifying, "I am in!"

Joseph, as a result of obeying heaven's angelic representative, likely became the subject of scandal and the butt of jokes from those who did not know the truth about Mary's pregnancy, experiencing the general censure of society. But he chose divine expediency over social acceptance and crowd approval to become the most famous stepfather in the world. Through it all, he obeyed God and loved Mary. Let's hear it for Joseph, who had the intestinal fortitude to say, "I am in!"

Gabriel and the angelic choir obeyed God's instructions to bring His words to various human beings who were central to His Kingdom plan, and they glorified Him. Each was affirming to the Lord, concerning the restoration of His Kingdom on earth and in the hearts of human beings worldwide, "We're in!"

Simeon and Anna, the aged ones, were among those who, hoping against hope, were expecting the Messiah, and they joined in welcoming

Him at His birth. When Simeon recognized the baby Jesus as the Christ and began to pray, he was certainly exclaiming in his heart, "Of course, I have been in for years!" And when Anna broke into thanksgiving, she was surely affirming the same.

Simply reading and taking note of the cluster of decisions and miraculous events we've just discussed ignites a fire of amazement and wonder in me at Jesus' history-shaping birth. Each act, word, and incident—together—form a chain of evidence that brings the world into a mode of eternal hope. It remains the world's only hope.

How the Kingdom Comes

Now, the big question for us: this being a picture of how the Kingdom came through a baby in a manger and His mother, how does the Kingdom come to us today? What do the experiences of the first-century players reveal to us? What will give the Kingdom a voice and feet to fulfill this astounding and daring promise that Jesus gave near the end of His ministry?

> *This good news of the Kingdom will be proclaimed in all the world as a testimony to all nations. And then the end will come.*
>
> (Matthew 24:14)

You may have noticed that I haven't yet specifically summarized Mary's part in the story. That is because I have been saving her for now. Without argument, Mary plays the leading human role in this cosmic drama, and she is the prime model for us today of how to welcome the Kingdom into our world. All the other players in the drama were highly significant. Each of them made a vital contribution in the re-establishment of the Kingdom of heaven on earth, and they experienced both its power and protocol amid an insurgent, rebellious earth. They deserve our honor and attention, because their faith and obedience paved the way for the Kingdom to come. However, none were as vital as Mary. The response of this young woman was the greatest factor in the execution of heaven's plan for earth to host its Creator-King and His Kingdom. Her body housed the life of God in human form, and it was to her (along with Joseph) that Jesus' care was entrusted during His childhood and young adulthood.

Mary, the Primary Model

Who Is Mary?

Meet Mary, the most famous woman in human history and surely among the most adored. For centuries, Mary's role has been much discussed throughout the world, her importance a subject of heated debate as well as lavish admiration. In the end, she is a model of obedience and faithfulness, a position we must all take to accommodate the plans for the advancement of the Kingdom of God for the remainder of our lives on earth.

> *Mary's response was the greatest factor in the execution of heaven's plan for earth to host its Creator-King and His Kingdom.*

To provide some background to our discussion of Mary, I want to share with you what I believe was a Kingdom sighting or affirmation in relation to the importance of our theme in this chapter. In December 2015, my wife, Friede, and I had just returned from twelve days of ministry. We gathered up the massive bundle of mail that had accumulated in our absence and hauled it with our luggage into our condo. In the mail was that month's issue of *National Geographic*, a magazine I have subscribed to for many years. My heart skipped a beat when I took the magazine out of its plastic sleeve, and lo and behold, there on the cover was a full-page painting depicting the face of Mary the mother of Jesus. The title, in large white letters, was "Mary," with the subtitle "The Most Powerful Woman in the World." I was in minor shock, knowing that, in light of what I was writing about Mary and the Kingdom for this book, this was beyond mere coincidence.

I was also surprised over the fact that *National Geographic*, a highly respected secular periodical whose staff might own the title of "progressive" or "liberal," and might espouse evolution and Aristotelian thinking, would focus on Mary, the most famous woman in the Bible. More amazing than that was the fact that the article under discussion was the lead article characterized by journalistic excellence in a magazine highly valued by the scientific community. This splendid article was, appropriately, designed to appear at Christmastime, when songs about Mary were being heard and sung around the world, artistic renderings of her on Christmas cards were being distributed, and manger scenes featuring replicas of Mary, Joseph, and the Christ Child were being displayed everywhere.

Several pages into the magazine was a brief word by Susan Goldberg, editor in chief, with an explanation about the lead article, which came later in the magazine. In her editorial piece, entitled "Hail Mary," she referenced an exhibition a year prior in Washington, DC, at the National Museum of Women in the Arts, which had featured seventy-four pieces of art under the title "Picturing Mary: Woman, Mother, Idea." The artworks were from the fourteenth through the nineteenth centuries, on loan from several galleries of renown in Florence, Paris, and Rome. The event had drawn the largest exhibition attendance ever for the museum. This fact caused the staff of *National Geographic* to wonder what the huge interest in this ancient woman Mary was all about. The magazine sent Maureen Orth, who wrote the story on Mary, with a photographer around the globe in search of "explanations and insights" as to what makes Mary, of biblical fame, deserving of the title "The Most Powerful Woman in the World" today.

Susan Goldberg continued her comments with references to Mary as a woman whose powers are invoked by a variety of people, including the sick, mothers, professional football quarterbacks, and truckers. Her observation at the end of the editorial introducing the splendid report was, "There's a unifying power in the faith that Mary inspires in so many. And that, it could be argued, is in itself something of a miracle."

In the lead article, Mary is boldly acknowledged as the "Virgin Mary" without further discussion. The article is almost thirty pages long, with several thousand words of prose and fifteen pictures, some spanning two pages, from across the world where many "Mary sightings" or apparitions have been reported, along with thousands of healings claimed along the way, from Mexico, Bosnia, France, Italy, India, Philippines, and Africa. The reports in the article indicate the cautionary approach of the Catholic Church to confirm the many sightings, prophetic messages, and healings as valid. In Lourdes alone, the "Virgin's miracle factory," more than seven thousand miracles have been claimed since the mid-1800s, with sixty-nine having been recognized as valid by the Catholic Church.

As I read the article, I was still somewhat stunned, and my imagination was shattered. But it wasn't due to what you might think. In all likelihood, Mary is the most overlooked and unsung hero of the ages; at the same time, she is admired, adored, and yes, even worshipped by many. I have no desire to enter into the debate over the attention and honor that Mary has received. Mainly, I believe that the teachings of our Catholic friends that center on her are to the apparent neglect of the Christ child she bore. But what has blown me off the road temporarily is the overwhelming stir and attention this one great woman has brought to the whole world.

I am willing to repent of the mistake of not honoring Mary as much as she deserves for fear that I might be accused of worshipping her. A re-action against an inappropriate veneration of Mary is perhaps the reason that many of us have inadvertently denied her the honor she deserves, for fear of making her into an idol instead of recognizing her as an exception-al believer whose devotion to God should be imitated. Again, it must be recognized and remembered that this one teenage girl modeled a level of obedience that all of us need to emulate to accommodate the expansion of the Kingdom of God in the twenty-first century.

Mary's Response to God

With this as background, let us now return to the Luke narrative, to the epic episode where the angel Gabriel appears to Mary. This encoun-ter is part of the greatest story ever told; it influences every event, phase, and construct in history. Whomever and whatever God was looking for to be the primary hostess of the life of God in human form, He found in this young woman. Thus, we may, with a great deal of safety and like-lihood, and with an accompanying degree of satisfaction, find in Mary some secrets regarding how the Kingdom came in Jesus' day—and how the Kingdom comes in our day. Her story, in itself, might well be entitled "How the Kingdom Came."

The angel Gabriel approaches Mary with the salutation, *"Rejoice, favored woman! The Lord is with you"* (Luke 1:28). Unsurprisingly, Mary was troubled, *"wondering what kind of greeting this could be"* (verse 29).

Dear reader, take a deep breath and remember you are witnessing the unfolding of the greatest drama in history, which would define time itself and become a story familiar to many of the more than seven billion people on earth. Please allow yourself to be astonished that what you are about to read really took place in real time between a real teenage woman and an angel sent from heaven's throne, from the heart of God. This conversation between heaven and earth is of cosmic significance, and it affects you and me, even at this present moment.

The angel Gabriel continues,

> *"Do not be afraid, Mary, for you have found favor with God. Now listen: You will conceive and give birth to a son, and you will call His name Jesus. He will be great and will be called the Son of the Most High, and the Lord will give Him the throne of His father David. He will reign over the house of Jacob forever, and His Kingdom will have no end." Mary asked the angel, "How can this be, since I have not been intimate with a man?" The angel replied to her: "The Holy Spirit will come upon you, and the power of the Most High will overshadow you. Therefore, the holy One to be born will be called the Son of God. And consider your relative Elizabeth—even she has conceived a son in her old age, and this is the sixth month for her who was called childless. For nothing will be impossible with God."* (Luke 1:30–37)

Never before and never again will human ears hear a statement like this, nor will there ever be the need for such. This was the herald of the reestablishment of the Kingdom of God on earth. Mary's response to the Lord and His Word confirms the validity of His choice in selecting her to be the mother of the Son of God, to be the human component of the majestic miracle of the incarnation—God becoming man. Here is her response:

I am the servant of the Lord; let it be to me according to your word.

(Luke 1:38 ESV)

With this answer, reflecting a heart of devotion to God, Mary cooperated with the Lord in an incomparable mystery as He, through her, effected the incarnation and the return of the Kingdom on earth. She also accepted the fact that people would probably judge her, but she was willing to experience the severest of human scorn and rejection. Once more, she deserves our honor and our high appraisal.

Mary's Qualities

Let's look at a list of Mary's qualities that challenge us and indicate our own potential—we in whom Christ is being formed for a watching world to see.

First, we may assume that Mary, like her relative Elizabeth, knew the Old Testament Scriptures and lived in such a manner as to be obedient to them. Remember that it was said of Elizabeth (and of Zechariah) that she lived *"without blame according to all the commandments and requirements of the Lord"* (Luke 1:6). By inference, we may safely assume the same of Mary, as she was chosen as God's instrument and is described by the angel as having *"found favor with God"* (Luke 1:30).

> *We must learn to listen to, hear, and heed the Word of God.*

Second, she who would be the bearer of the Son of God was surely a listener for and to the revelatory word of God. This whole narrative centers on and issues from that word.

Third, she heard the word from God. Listening is necessary to hearing. The probability is that most of us do not have a hearing problem as much as a listening problem. By habit, Mary was both a listener and a hearer, as we will observe more fully later. We, too, are never to stop our pursuit of the Word of God; we must listen, hear, and heed, as Mary so aptly models for us.

Fourth, Mary received the Word. When she asked the angel, *"How can this be?"* (Luke 1:34), her reply did not indicate disbelief. Her inquiry had to do with "how" this amazing thing could happen. Her virginity notwithstanding, when the how was stated to her in general terms, she replied, *"I am the servant of the Lord; let it be to me according to your word"* (Luke 1:38 ESV).

This is too huge a response to pass over lightly. It is the epicenter of this extraordinary episode. The incarnation could never have occurred apart from Mary's powerful affirmation. She was saying, in effect, "I don't have a clue as to how this is exactly going to come about, but I do know that I am alive to serve God…let it be as you have said!" It is my studied opinion that at this very moment, in the fullness of time, as Mary sounded the words *"Let it be to me,"* the Holy Spirit planted the Word of God in her womb, and she was suddenly pregnant as the divine sperm met Mary's egg.

Luke 8:11, which is part of the parable of the sower, says, *"The seed is the word of God."* I think it is both deeply interesting and highly significant that in this verse, the Greek word for *"seed"* is *sporos*, a term that is related to *sperma*. In the eternal dynamics of the mystery of the incarnation, time and eternity, flesh and spirit, collided—and a virgin impregnated by God's "seed" became the vehicle through which God's eternal Word became the long-promised Messiah!

Again, stop here, take a deep breath, and whisper to yourself, "This truly happened in real time!" Then ask God to begin to reveal to you the eternal, universal, and all-inclusive implications of this episode for all of time and eternity. At the moment, I feel like Moses must have felt when God said, "Take off your shoes, you're standing on holy ground." (See Exodus 3:5.)

Fifth, Mary believed the Word she had received. Note carefully the sequence of events. Mary said, *"Let it be to me according to your word!"* At that moment, the conversation was finished and the mission completed; the angel left her, and Mary was already pregnant! How do we know? Read on!

In those days Mary set out and hurried to a town in the hill country of Judah where she entered Zechariah's house and greeted Elizabeth.
(Luke 1:39–40)

Again, let's slow down here to take it all in. Why did Mary go to the home of Zechariah and Elizabeth? No doubt, it was due to the information Gabriel had revealed to her about Elizabeth: *"And consider your relative Elizabeth—even she has conceived a son in her old age, and this is the sixth month for her who was called childless. For nothing will be impossible with God"* (Luke 1:36–37). In Elizabeth, Mary had someone with whom she could share her news and discuss the angel's visit.

What happened next is worthy of all our attention. The moment Elizabeth heard Mary's greeting, something happened in Elizabeth's body: *"the baby leaped inside her, and Elizabeth was filled with the Holy Spirit"* (Luke 1:41).

Now carefully observe what Elizabeth said to Mary,

You are the most blessed of women, and your child will be blessed! How could this happen to me, that the mother of my Lord should come to me? For you see, when the sound of your greeting reached my ears, the baby leaped for joy inside me! She who has believed is blessed because what was spoken to her by the Lord will be fulfilled! (Luke 1:42–45)

Do you see what is happening here? We are witnessing a supernatural exchange, an air-tight, mutual confirmation that Mary is pregnant.

Sixth, Mary confessed the word. Her supernatural response to Elizabeth's revelation was nothing short of a word of knowledge by the Holy Spirit. In this breathtaking drama, Mary breaks into song. The most important issues in this glorious, unparalleled, ten-verse shout of praise called the "Magnificat" is that it is a confession that she is pregnant, and that it reveals to her that she has been scripted into God's cosmic plan for eternity. But this was not just a word from Mary to Elizabeth; it was the word of God through Mary to the whole world. In this light, what happened next was a vital component of Mary's Kingdom protocol.

I cannot resist including these words, which are among the grandest of time and eternity, straight from the throne of heaven through Mary's heart and lips:

> *My soul proclaims the greatness of the Lord, and my spirit has rejoiced in God my Savior, because He has looked with favor on the humble condition of His slave. Surely, from now on all generations will call me blessed, because the Mighty One has done great things for me, and His name is holy. His mercy is from generation to generation on those who fear Him. He has done a mighty deed with His arm; He has scattered the proud because of the thoughts of their hearts; He has toppled the mighty from their thrones and exalted the lowly. He has satisfied the hungry with good things and sent the rich away empty. He has helped his servant Israel, mindful of His mercy, just as He spoke to our ancestors, to Abraham and his descendants forever.* (Luke 1:46–55)

Let's summarize thus far Mary's protocol in relation to how the Kingdom came:

1. She lived in such a way that she knew God's Word and was within sound of His revelatory word.

2. She listened to God's word.

3. She heard the word.

4. She received the word.

5. She believed the word.

6. She confessed the word.

Now, there is one other vital component in the continuum of this cosmic drama:

7. Mary *remembered* the word.

This last aspect is essential. The validation of the whole scenario is that Mary's whole life, not just at the moment when she accepted God's assignment, was centered on the Word and words of God. For the months before and after Jesus' birth, and for years afterward, she pondered and confirmed all that she had heard from the Lord. For example, when Jesus was born, the shepherds witnessed the choir of angels and the glory of God, being terrified by it all, and heard angelic voices saying, *"Don't be afraid, for look, I proclaim to you good news of great joy"* (Luke 2:10), and *"Glory to God in the highest heaven, and peace on earth to people He favors"* (verse 14). They conveyed this information to Joseph and Mary when they went to visit the newborn Messiah, and then to others. (See Luke 2:16–18.) Note Mary's response to all the collateral excitement that surrounded the birth:

> But Mary was treasuring up all these things in her heart and meditating on them. (Luke 2:19)

What intensifies the significance of this verse is the fact that the word here for *"things"* is *rhema*, one of the Greek terms translated "word" in the New Testament! The issue with Mary was still the words of God. She was pondering them and meditating on them. Thus, for thirty years following His birth, Jesus lived, from infancy to manhood, in an atmosphere charged with the presence of God, where God's words were central and He was honored as King. It was in this atmosphere that Jesus *"became strong, filled with wisdom, and God's grace was on Him"* (Luke 2:40).

> *Growing up, Jesus lived in an atmosphere charged with God's presence, where God's words were central and He was honored as King.*

We see Mary's continued meditation on God's word after the incident when the twelve-year-old Jesus went missing during the family's journey home from the Passover Festival in Jerusalem. At this discovery, Mary and Joseph had been plunged into unimaginable panic. They had finally found

Jesus after days of searching, locating Him in the temple complex, calmly sitting among the teachers, listening to them and giving insightful answers to their questions. This is when Mary asked, in exasperation, *"Son, why have You treated us like this? Your father and I have been anxiously searching for You"* (Luke 2:48).

As we discussed earlier, Jesus' calm reply was, *"Why were you searching for me? Didn't you know that I had to be in My Father's house?"* (Luke 2:49). Neither Mary nor Joseph fully understood what He meant, but they went back to Nazareth together, Jesus walking with them. The Scriptures say that, following this rather dramatic incident, *"His mother kept all these things in her heart"* (Luke 2:51). Again, the word for *"things"* is *rhema*. God's word was still her daily fare.

We may assume that for the next eighteen years before Jesus' ministry began, the protocol of Mary and Joseph was consistent with this as they lived in the same house with the Son of God in amazement and mystery. In my opinion, Mary's habit of "pondering all these things," or words, from God, continued steadily through the perilous, fearful, and mystifying days of Jesus' ministry amid the fierce and increasing opposition of the religious establishment, His general rejection from virtually every venue of society and probably even from members of His own family, and His crucifixion at the hands of the Roman government. She felt the hurt deeply, striving constantly to achieve a balance in relating to her Son as both a human being and the divine Savior, all the while the crosswinds of popular opinion were blowing in her face.

Apparently, there is not one piece of evidence, throughout the whole trying experience, that she wavered in the slightest sense from what she heard from God through His angel when she was a teenage girl, and from what she said in reply. And, through it all, she surely continued to "ponder all these things in her heart." Then, as the apex of the cosmic drama drew near, and she stood as close to the cross as she dared, watching her own Son suffer as no human has ever suffered or ever will suffer, the blood dripping from His wounds from head to foot, she still pondered. Add to this the mocking crowd, the soldiers of the Roman guard showing no mercy, recklessly joking beneath the cross, inflicting more innovations of misery,

Mary's heartache was made all the more indescribable—and still she pondered without wavering.

She heard the cries of her Son, just before He died, and the words He spoke to her and His disciple John, "*Woman, here is your son*" (John 19:26), and "*Here is your mother*" (verse 27). She pondered still.

And for the years to come, that same commitment to God and His Word proved be a blessed life sentence. It never ceased—through thick and thin, pain and loss, mystery and perplexity. It continued through Jesus' life and ministry, His death and resurrection, His final days on earth, His ascension into heaven, and the birth of the church. It will prove wise for us to follow her example, meditating on the words, works, and ways of God as He restores His eternal Kingdom on earth.

Receiving the Challenge; Praying the Prayer

Is it too audaciously simple to believe that the same protocol applies to us today as the one Mary and the other players in the cosmic drama demonstrated in the first century? No, this is how the Kingdom came, and this is precisely how the Kingdom comes today—through faith, obedience, a devotion to God's Word and words, and a full embrace of His purposes. Will you adopt this protocol by saying "Yes!" to the King and His Kingdom? The decision is yours and mine—individually, at first; and then eventually in a corporate sense, as the church.

It has been twenty centuries since Jesus' birth, marking the re-beginning of the Kingdom of God on earth. We make much of the beginning without being very aware of its implications. There is now among us on earth the Spirit of Him who was born on that day long ago in a manger. At the same time, His Spirit inhabits each of us who name and receive Him as Savior and Lord. As surely as these monumental facts are true, there is a construct, real but invisible, called the Kingdom of God, that is with us, around us, and in us, exercising a unique and powerful influence. There is also the church, not an agency or an institution but a living, breathing organism of all believers in Jesus, throbbing with divine life, that serves to represent the eternal reign of God on earth, and spiritually holds the balance of power in the world.

Because we believe the gospel narrative regarding the coming of the Christ to this earth to establish a visible colony of the eternal and invisible Kingdom, we stand firm and fixed behind a totally optimistic view of the ultimate future of this planet and of the entire universe. What started early in the first century is still in our midst today and will remain and thrive until the end of the age. As I have expressed, the message and might of the narrative of the Kingdom of God is being sounded with increasing passion and frequency throughout the world.

This church is about to experience the recovery of the Kingdom gospel with Kingdom power and Kingdom love, and with all this will come the Kingdom harvest. The eternal Kingdom of God was launched on earth by divine decree with the authority and potency to rearrange the culture, first within believers, then around us to the world, until righteousness covers the earth as the waters cover the sea. The power to accomplish this is here among us and within us to operate to the glory of God.

Like Mary, you may ask, "How...?" The answer is the same: "'*The Holy Spirit will come upon you, and the power of the Most High will overshadow you.*' For no Word from God is without power!" (See Luke 1:35, 37.) That last sentence is a literal translation of the phrase "*for nothing will be impossible with God*" (verse 37).

Your answer and mine must be the same as Mary's: "*May it be done to me according to Your word*" (Luke 1:38).

Mary, our model of obedience and cooperation, said to the Lord, "I'm in!"

Will you do the same?

Let's call the roll:

Gabriel's response: "I'm in!"

Zechariah's response: "I'm in!"

Elizabeth's response: "I'm in!"

Joseph's response: "I'm in!"

Mary's response: "I'm in!"

Simeon's response: "I'm in!"

Anna's response: "I'm in!"

My response, "I'm in!"

Your response? Read the rest and then record your decision:

_____.

If what you have read in this book is real at all, the Kingdom of God encompasses all the truth about everything, everybody, everywhere, in all of time and eternity. If it matters at all, it is all that matters. I have emphasized in many different ways that the Kingdom of God, as ultimate reality, is "everything." Thus, it is the Kingdom of God or nothing! The eternal Kingdom of God is our reason for being, our reason for living, and our reason for believing.

The model prayer that Jesus gave us in Matthew 6 embraces the essence of God's nature and Kingdom, of man's relationship with God, of God's will for man, and of man's total need. To acknowledge the validity of this prayer is not a mere affirmation of the existence of God and His Kingdom but an all-out commitment to become a part of the eternal narrative into which we have been scripted. It is affirming loudly to God, "I am in!" Therefore, as we conclude our time together, my challenge to you is to read and speak aloud the following words, which, again, frame the essence of the model prayer in Matthew 6. *Listen* carefully to the words as you speak them aloud.

> *Your kingdom come. Your will be done on earth as it is in heaven.*
>   (Matthew 6:10)

Now you have a threefold witness of the words that express the heart of the greatest prayer ever prayed:

Witness One: You saw it.

Witness Two: You said it.

Witness Three: You heard it.

Now, I am asking you today to do one other thing: mean it! To pray this prayer is to accept a life calling of seeking the Kingdom above every other pursuit. The facts that you have read this book and also spoken this prayer are evidence that you acknowledge this Kingdom, this prayer, and these truths as eternally valid.

Now, it's just you and God and these words. Will you whisper to Him, "Father, whatever You are up to, I am in!"? Say those nine words, and then reiterate the last three: "I am in!"

Careful now, can you mean it with all your heart? Then *pray* it slowly:

Father, I am in; Your Kingdom come, Your will be done, on earth as it is in heaven.

Did you notice that I said "pray," when before I said "say"? It is one thing to say something; it is quite another to pray it. In the former, you are just speaking words; in the latter, you are communicating with God. He alone knows whether or not you mean what you say; but in all likelihood, either way, He will act on what you ask as if you really meant it. My dear friend, if you will do what I have asked you to do, I guarantee you one thing: something terribly wonderful and wonderfully terrible is about to happen in your life. You have my word on it, and I allow you to make me accountable to you.

To Be Continued...

This book has not been written, nor the story told, merely as a lesson to be believed. It is to be received and acted upon in continuing commitment, modeled by the cast of characters in the drama of the ages, principally by Mary, the mother of Jesus, who said, *"May it be done to me according to Your word"* (Luke 1:38). As these words passed Mary's lips, in effect, she received the King and His Kingdom. Celebrate the result of that moment with me:

For a child will be born for us, a son will be given to us, and the government will be on His shoulders. He will be named Wonderful Counselor, Mighty God, Eternal Father, Prince of Peace. The dominion will
be vast, and its prosperity will **never end**. He will reign on the throne
of David and over his Kingdom, to establish and sustain it with justice

and righteousness from now on and forever. The zeal of the LORD of Hosts will accomplish this. (Isaiah 9:6–7)

I almost wrote "The End" here, until the bolded words in the above passage stood out to me, and writing such words seemed prohibitive. Therefore, instead of "The End," I write:

To Be Continued...FOREVER!

A PARTING PERSONAL PROPHECY

At first, it seemed strange to me to include this personal prophecy at the end of *Cosmic Initiative*, but after some thought, I knew it was something I had to do. Here it is:

> You will experience a moment that will jog your memory about something you have read in this book. It may come in moments, days, months, or years after reading it. When that happens, you will know that these words are for you.
>
> You will have a Kingdom confrontation, and at that precise moment, you will look forward to the rest of your life and make a decision that will affect every venue of your life from that moment on.
>
> God will remind you of the price demanded for the Kingdom life, and for a long moment you will ponder more deeply than ever before the demands of Kingdom-centeredness and heaven's control. You will either quietly choose to go on with business as usual, or you will say (and mean) the words that altered the lives of all involved in the narrative of the Kingdom:
>
> "I'm in!"

Then, and only then, will you know and begin to understand that the Kingdom is both the pearl of great price and the treasure in the field, and those brief words will open for you HEAVEN ON EARTH!

Please know you have been prayed for!

—*Jack Taylor*
Dimensions Ministries
Melbourne, Florida

APPENDIX: A PREMIUM POEM WITH AN ADDENDUM

The following is one of the most intriguing poems I have ever read, and I wanted to include it as an addendum to this book because it highlights the fact that the eternal Kingdom is "everything." The central theme chronicled throughout this sad poem is the fact that nothing here on earth lasts, whether sorrow or joy, tragedy or triumph, defeat or victory. The words that close each stanza, "Even this shall pass away," strike me with a strange sadness, and I weep every time I read them. I wondered why until I saw the eternal Kingdom of God as the ultimate answer to this sadness and was moved to add the words that appear following the last stanza. As far as I am concerned, this last thought changes the tragedy of time itself. Read it and encounter something that never ceases to be!

The King's Ring[34]

Once in Persia reigned a king,
Who, upon his signet-ring

---

34. Theodore Tilton, "The King's Ring." There have been various versions of this poem through the years. The original was published in 1858. (I prefer the title "A Kingdom Poem on the Ring of the King.")

Graved a maxim true and wise,
Which, if held before his eyes
Gave good counsel, at a glance,
Fit for every change or chance:
Solemn words, and these are they:
"Even this shall pass away!"

Trains of camels through the sand
Brought him gems from Samarcand.
Fleets of galleys through the seas
Brought him pearls to rival these.
But he counted little gain
Treasures of the mine and main.
"What is wealth?" the king would say,
"Even this shall pass away!"

In the revels of his court
At the zenith of his sport,
When the palms of all his guests,
Burned with clapping at his jests,
He, amid his figs and wine,
Cried, "O loving friends of mine,
Pleasure comes but not to stay,
"Even this shall pass away."

Lady fairest ever seen
Was the bride he crowned his queen.
Pillowed on the marriage-bed,
Whispering to his soul, he said,
"Though a bridegroom never pressed
Greater beauty to his breast,
Mortal flesh must come to clay:
"Even this shall pass away."

Fighting on a furious field,
Once a javelin pierced his shield

Soldiers with a loud lament
Bore him bleeding to his tent.
Groaning from his tortured side,
"Pain is hard to bear!" He cried.
"But with patience day by day,
Even this shall pass away."

Towering in the public square,
Twenty cubits in the air,
Rose his statue carved in stone.
Then the king, disguised, unknown,
Gazing at his sculptured name,
Asked himself, "And what is fame?
Fame is but a slow decay,
Even his shall pass away."

Struck with palsy, sore and old,
Waiting at the gates of gold,
Spake he at his dying breath,
"Life is done, but what is death?"
Then, in answer to the king,
Fell a sunbeam on his ring,
Showing by a heavenly ray,
"Even this shall pass away."

A sad sort of poem deserves a better, gladder ending. This is my offering:

We have seen the worst, the best,
Now to face the final test.
Death looms large and bids our plea,
"What is left in life for me?"
Not to look to ancient ring,
But to words from THE great King:
"Look to *My* Kingdom this day,
IT SHALL NEVER PASS AWAY!"

ANNOTATED KINGDOM BIBLIOGRAPHY

The Bible, Our Premium Source and Guide: A Tribute and a Determination

As we study the Kingdom of God, we must never forget that our premium source is the Bible. It is literally the manual of the Kingdom. Whatever we read about the Kingdom apart from the Bible must be confirmed, certified, and ratified in this, the Word of God. Let's make the following confession together. Take your Bible in hand and declare with me:

This is my Bible. It contains the Word of God and is the Word of God.

It is not only filled with miracles; it is a miracle.

It is a miracle in its origination, or *inspiration*: This is that work of the Spirit of God in men of God who made their writings a record of divine revelation.

It is a miracle in it continuation, or *preservation*: This is that work of the Spirit of God on the translations and the translators themselves that guaranteed the arrival of the Bible in every successive generation with its originally-intended message intact.

It is a miracle in its present revelation, or *illumination*: This is that work of the Spirit of God in the lives of its readers, students, and teachers that makes the present experience one of divine exchange.

THIS IS MY BIBLE.

IT IS INFALLIBLE, CREDIBLE, AND RELIABLE.

IT IS THE DISTILLATION OF THE BREATH OF GOD IN PRINT.

BECAUSE OF THE WORK OF THE SPIRIT OF GOD, IT HAS PRESENT POWER TO EFFECT CHANGE IN ALL WHO HEAR IT, READ IT, QUOTE IT, PREACH IT, AND OBEY IT.

THE SAME SPIRIT THAT INSPIRED IT AND PRESERVED IT NOW LIVES IN ME TO ILLUMINATE IT.

ALL THAT I READ OF THE KINGDOM ELSEWHERE WILL BE MONITORED, JUDGED, CLARIFIED, VALIDATED, AND EMPOWERED BY THE SPIRIT OF GOD TO BE SCRIPTURAL OR TO BE DISCOUNTED.

IN JESUS' NAME, AMEN!

Kingdom Bibliography

I have a large section on the Kingdom of God in my working library. For me, seeking the Kingdom has become a happy obsession. I add to this treasure trove all the time. For the greater part of two decades, I have found myself reading either a new passage of Kingdom-enlightened revelation in the Bible, a new Kingdom book, or an old book that always yields new light on the Kingdom. About the time I get a hint that I know something regarding God's Kingdom, I see a new vista that stretches my soul, challenges my spirit, and activates my adrenal gland. At those times, I am reminded that comparing what I know to what there is to know, my knowledge is fractional, indeed. I have the distinct feeling that when the great transition from earth to glory suddenly takes place, I will be heard shouting, as did Sheba's queen, "The half was never told!" (See 1 Kings 10:7.)

Top Ten Kingdom Books for Review and Study

The following is not nearly a full list of great Kingdom books but rather those that have had—and are having—a continuing influence on my pursuit of Kingdom truth. Instead of a standard bibliography, I have chosen to make a list of the books on the Kingdom with notes as to why and how they might be influential in future studies of the subject on the part of my readers. These reports are of a personal nature and are not intended to be agreed with apart from your own experience. Please do not be bothered if you do not concur. Remember, this is my personal position.

I have limited this first list to ten books so as not to confuse those planning a life study of this vital subject. My prayers for you who have not yet caught the Kingdom virus is that you will be infected and become infectious—so infectious that others will become highly infected and infectious, too!

These first ten authors and their works are in a category I have labeled the "greatest," which again is simply my personal opinion and experience. You should not try to read any of these books rapidly but rather carefully. I have included the most recent publication information where possible.

1. Jones, E. Stanley. *The Unshakable Kingdom and the Unchanging Person*. New York: Dutton, 1958.

This is the *greatest entry-level* book on the Kingdom in print and is an easy read, divided into bite-sized paragraphs for a pleasant experience, and making for clearer understanding. Simple yet profound, the reader will be more likely to "get it" on the first read than not. A book to return to again and again. I have worn out three copies, read it often, and refer to it repeatedly. My organization has distributed thousands of them.

2. Boardman, George Dana. *The Kingdom: The Emerging Order of Christ Among Men*. Shippensburg, PA: Destiny Image Publishers, 2008.

This book is an amazing work published in 1899 and is, in my opinion, the *greatest exegetical book* on the Kingdom of God in print. It is written in a style so pleasant and brilliant that one tends to feel the heart of the author in his very usage of words. Boardman was pastor of the First Baptist Church of Philadelphia, Pennsylvania, from 1865 to1895. His father served as an associate of the great missionary statesman Adoniram Judson of Burma. Couched in beautiful prose and powerfully illustrated, it is a book resurrected from anonymity to bless a new generation. A must for every believer seeking the Kingdom.

3. Willard, Dallas. *The Divine Conspiracy*. New York: HarperCollins, 2014 (originally published in 1998).

An amazing book from the heart of a tenured and adored professor of philosophy at the University of Southern California until his death in 2014. In my thinking, this the *greatest book for a unique combination of simplicity, breadth, depth, and warmth*. Richard Foster, in his moving foreword to this book, says, "This is the book I have been searching for all my life. If the *parousia* tarries, his is a book for the next millennium."

My copy of Willard's book is one to which I have returned many times, and it looks ancient from so much marking and wear. To me, the richness of the book is embellished by the fact that I spoke to him briefly as he lay on the sickbed from which he changed locations to the other side of the Kingdom. If there is a familiar ring to the title of the book you are reading, I am happy to tell you that I discussed this matter with Jane, Dallas's widow, who happily approved my title and voiced a hope that *Divine Conspiracy* could experience a rush of fresh interest because of this book. It belongs in every believer's library.

4. Hetland, Leif. *Seeing Through Heaven's Eyes*. Shippensburg, PA: Destiny Image Publishers, 2011.

This man and this book are destined to change the world. Leif is a cherished and celebrated son of mine and has written the *greatest book on Kingdom love and Kingdom thinking*. The book is not yet well known, but it will be as people meet Leif, encounter the title, read the book, and find alignment and assignment in the Kingdom of God. A native of Norway, Leif Hetland is rapidly finding a place in the world as an apostle of love, a title given him in Pakistan by leaders of Islam, which is an amazing story in itself, soon to be told. Read *Through Heaven's Eyes* and return to it often.

5. Munroe, Myles. *Rediscovering the Kingdom* (expanded edition, 2010), *God's Big Idea* (2008), *Applying the Kingdom* (2007), *Kingdom Principles* (2006), all published by Destiny Image, Shippensburg, PA, and others from Myles Munroe's fleet of great Kingdom books.

Together, these volumes win the title of the *greatest books for practical understanding and application on the subject of the Kingdom*. Myles Munroe was a brilliant author who published many more books than those listed above. Growing up and living in the Bahamas, which was once an island colony of Britain, he was familiar with the nature, purpose, and protocol of an earthly kingdom and its colonies. He had a level of understanding that exploded with implications in regard to earth being a colony of heaven. Myles Munroe's books make up a vital section in my library. Myles, his wife, and seven others met a seemingly untimely death in 2014 flying in a private plane from Nassau to Freeport, Grand Bahama island, for an annual leadership conference. I wept and wondered and wonder still.

6. Ladd, George Eldon. *The Presence of the Future*. Grand Rapids: Eerdmans, 1996.

This may be a surprise, but I was first drawn to uncommon interest in the Kingdom of God by reading this book. For me it is the *greatest **seminal** book* on the Kingdom of God I have read. By that, I mean it is like a seed, a beginning, a source that proves its worth as time goes on. It brings new meaning to the "aha!" phase of study on the Kingdom. It was with "Uncle George" that I was injected with the Kingdom "virus." The greatness of this book is enhanced by two of his other books, *The Gospel of the Kingdom* (1968) and *Crucial Questions About the Kingdom of God* (1952), both also published by Eerdmans.

7. Johnson, Bill. *When Heaven Invades Earth*. Shippensburg, PA: Destiny Image Publishers, 2005.

In my view, this amazing book wins the award as being the *greatest articulation of the inexorable results of the Kingdom message, i.e., the invasion of heaven's influence in blending the **normal** with the **supernatural*** for God's program on planet Earth. Bill Johnson, another of my cherished and celebrated sons, stands, in my opinion, as a paragon of spiritual excellence and a unique combination of true greatness and humility. A plethora of strategic books have followed this one, including *The Supernatural Power of a Transformed Mind* (expanded edition, Destiny Image 2014), *Experience the Impossible* (Chosen Books, 2014), and *The Power that Changes the World* (Chosen Books, 2015).

8. Kendall, R. T. *The Sermon on the Mount*. Grand Rapids: Chosen Books, 2011. Also, *The Lord's Prayer*. London: Hodder & Stoughton, 2011.

These two books are the *greatest invitations to Kingdom living, Kingdom praying, and Kingdom thinking* I have read. Every book I have read from R.T.'s pen leaves me feeling that I have just experienced the ultimate word on the subject. This is one of the reasons why I have not delved into obvious facets of the Kingdom as R.T. and others have done. No one I know of at present is touching the world with Kingdom influence through speaking and writing as much as this amazing man. The width of his acceptance among evangelicals and charismatics, theologians and common folks, world leaders and obscure people, is an unexplainable phenomenon.

With Charles Carrin, R.T. and I have ministered together in more than seventy "Word Spirit & Power" conferences in Canada, England, and the United States in the past fifteen years. R.T. spends the first six months of the year ministering in England where, after finishing his education at Oxford, he was the beloved pastor of the Westminster Chapel in London, England. He is viewed by many as among the greatest living theologians, a view with which I heartily agree! He has written more than sixty books. He credits Charles Carrin, my next subject, with helping Westminster Chapel in London to become a church with a better balance of the entities of Word and Spirit.

9. Carrin, Charles. *The Edge of Glory*. Lake Mary, FL: Creation House, 2002.

This man, my friend and colleague, is one if the greatest thinkers I have ever known. He has written in this book *the greatest challenge to move from common Christianity to a life of releasing the Spirit and living in Kingdom power.* I readily and happily include Charles in this list and recommend this book to everyone who desires to walk out the will and life of God on the earth. Herein are the theological underpinnings of such a protocol. His booklets, *Sunrise of David, Sunset of Saul,* and *On Whose Authority?* (available through Burkhart Books), the latter being a stern confrontation to those who seek to remove unwanted Scriptures from the Bible, are also must-reads. Find this man and his books, and you will have found treasures for life.

10. Billheimer, Paul E. *Destined for the Throne.* Bloomington, MN: Bethany House, 2005 (originally published in 1975).

This little book is easy to overlook; it is small, but it packs a wallop! I have read the book and also met the author. It is the *greatest challenge to discover the dynamics of prayer in training for eternal reigning.* I first visited with Paul and his wife, Ginny, many years ago after they moved to Atlanta to a humble little cottage in the woods just outside the city. They were already up in years then, and both of them were almost completely disabled. They had come there to die. But when this significant book was released, the message went viral, and God breathed new life into both Paul and Ginny. Paul had experienced a total physical breakdown a few years prior to this, but his mind and body rose to the challenges, and for the next several years, he and Ginny taught the contents of this book over Trinity Broadcasting Network regularly. I was asked to preach at Ginny's funeral and would have preached at "Pop" Billheimer's funeral had I not been out of the country. His other books have also wielded a mighty influence to this day: *Don't Waste Your Sorrows* (Bethany House, 2006); *Destined for the Cross* (Tyndale House, 1982); *Destined to Overcome* (Bethany House 2006); *Love Covers* (Christian Literature Crusade, 1974), and *Adventure in Adversity* (Tyndale House Publishers; 1984). Paul, being dead, yet speaks in these volumes. (See Hebrews 11:4.)

Ten Additional Great Kingdom Books

I have walked back and forth in my library, touching hundreds of volumes on the subject of the Kingdom of God with a sense that I will likely feel like kicking myself if I do not mention some additional splendid books that deserve a place in your library and in your spirit. Here are a few more titles, with brief comments.

11. Capon, Robert Farrar. *Kingdom, Grace, Judgment*. Grand Rapids: Eerdmans, 2002. This huge book is as significant as its size. Capon has seized the Kingdom with excitement and expectation and combines the material of several books on facets of the Kingdom message. His writing style is brilliant, and his disposition is feisty—a good mix for a scintillating read. Try him—you will like him!

12. Hylton, Jim. *The Supernatural Skyline: Where Heaven Touches Earth*. Shippensburg, PA: Destiny Image, 2010. A sure but novel presentation of the collateral dynamics of Kingdom appearances. Jim Hylton is a quiet and deep thinker among us. Read this one, and you'll want to read the one he's working on now—massive, unfinished, and as yet unnamed!

13. Jones, Martyn Lloyd. *The Kingdom of God*. Wheaton, IL: Crossway Books, 2010. A splendid series of expository sermons on the Kingdom and a refreshing experience to read. As I have walked back and forth among the volumes in my library, his works always catch my eye.

14. Kraybill, Donald B. *The Upside-Down Kingdom*. Harrisonburg, VA: Herald Press, 2011. A unique approach to the Kingdom of God in a "wrong-side up" society with an exhortation for believers to challenge the world system with Kingdom principles.

15. Leithart, Peter J. *The Kingdom and the Power*. Phillipsburg, NJ: P and R (Presbyterian and Reformed) Publishing, 1993. A strong rebuke against identifying the church and the Kingdom as one with the good news that the Kingdom alone can give the church its true identity.

16. Lewis, Charlie. *The Kingdom System: A Pattern for Guaranteed Success*, privately published, Maitland, FL: Xulon Press, 2013, and *Kingdomnomics: The Dynamics of Conduct and Behavior*, privately published, Charleston, SC: CreateSpace, 2015. These books come from a man who has sought and found the King and His Kingdom. He is a Kingdom man who runs a number of Kingdom businesses along with His wife, Fran. It is one thing to be a Christian businessman who believes in the Kingdom of God; it is quite another to be a Kingdom man whose businesses exist wholly for the glory of God. As God moves to restore the Kingdom message, might, and mentality to the church, He will place certain businessmen

strategically in the business world whose influence will be global. Charlie Lewis is one of those. Watch for him. As you do, read his books.

17. Moreland, J. P. *The Kingdom Triangle*. Grand Rapids, MI: Zondervan, 2007. A well-timed presentation for a messed-up society, showing the way out by the recovery of knowledge, the renovation of the soul, and the restoration of the Kingdom's miraculous power, a challenge both to society and to the church, with a foreword by Dallas Willard.

18. Vincent, Alan. *Heaven on Earth*. Shippensburg, PA: Destiny Image, 2008. A powerful challenge to receive and experience the supernatural Kingdom as a common and shared experience for all believers.

19. Watson, Thomas. *The Christian Soldier or Heaven Taken by Storm*. Charleston, SC: CreateSpace, 2014. Fresh light from two centuries ago on an ancient text about the Kingdom of heaven suffering violence.

20. Wimber, John. *Kingdom Mercy*. London: Hodder & Stoughton, 1988. This booklet is from a man who brought to a whole generation the refreshing message of the Kingdom of God, a man to whom we all owe much, and whose life and light have blessed all of us who knew him.

I will be mildly but pleasantly haunted by the thoughts of other books I should have recommended here, as well as other things I might have said or additional illustrations I could have presented in *Cosmic Initiative*. Yet there must be an end to all books, and that end has come. However, a happy thought has become a happy dance over the fact that, as we continue to learn, there will be even more books written as we seek to explore the unfathomable treasures of God's *Cosmic Initiative*.

ABOUT THE AUTHOR

Jack R. Taylor's name has become synonymous with the message of the Kingdom of God and the Spirit-filled life. He has been in ministry for more than sixty-five years and is not seeking retirement, believing his best years are still ahead of him.

Jack was saved at the age of ten and was called to preach at fourteen. Throughout his teen years, he preached in revivals, youth crusades, and local churches. Finishing high school before he was sixteen, he attended Hardin-Simmons University in Abilene, Texas, where he graduated in 1953 with a Bachelor of Arts degree, the youngest graduate in his class. After college, he enrolled in Southwestern Baptist Theological Seminary in Fort Worth and graduated with a Master of Divinity degree. In 1957, he was called to pastor Castle Hills First Baptist Church in San Antonio, Texas. During his nearly seventeen years there, the church grew from a membership of one hundred to over four thousand. In the 1970s, this church experienced a significant revival, with an estimated two thousand people saved in the first six months.

Jack served as pastoral advisor to the Conference of Southern Baptist Evangelists during the 1960s and 1970s. He was also elected first vice president of the Southern Baptist Convention in 1980. In addition, he has served on numerous boards, including that of Hardin-Simmons University, from which he was given the Distinguished Alumni Award in 1981. He also served on the board of *Fullness* magazine, where he was a major contributing author.

In 1974, Jack resigned as pastor to pursue itinerant ministry, and for more than forty years has served as president of Dimensions Ministries, headquartered in Melbourne, Florida. His experiences in the San Antonio revival launched him into a national and international ministry that has literally touched all corners of the globe. He has preached on five continents and in over sixty nations, including the United Kingdom, Spain, Germany, Austria, Russia, Liberia, Nigeria, Ghana, Ivory Coast, Kenya, Tanzania, Philippines, Greece, Israel, India, Indonesia, Singapore, Mexico, and Guatemala. In 1985, he launched AnchorChurch in Fort Worth, which he co-pastored with his son, Tim, until 1992. Today, he continues to preach in crusades, conferences, and churches throughout the United States and around the world.

Jack has two children, six grandchildren, and two great-grandchildren. He and his first wife, Barbara, were married for more than forty-seven years until she succumbed to cancer in 2001. In 2002, he married Jerry, who passed away after her own battle with cancer. Since 2004, Jack has been married to Friede, who travels and ministers with him. In 2009, they traveled more than two hundred and fifty thousand combined miles to serve the Lord around the world.

Jack received an honorary doctorate from St. Thomas College of Jacksonville, Florida, in 2011. He is currently working with his son, Tim, to develop Sonslink, a ministry committed to modeling the biblical Father/Son paradigm, with a growing network of spiritual sons and daughters across the world. For most of his ministry, Jack has instinctively fathered spiritual children in the ministry, counseling and encouraging young men and women to seek and expand the Kingdom of God; today, several hundred people formally consider Jack Taylor their spiritual father. Jack and Tim explore and expound on the Father/Son paradigm as the most significant relationship in the Kingdom of God, believing it to be the context for abundant living as well as Kingdom expansion.

In addition to *Cosmic Initiative*, his first book with Whitaker House, Jack is the author of thirteen other books, including the best-selling *The Key to Triumphant Living*, with one million copies in print.

Psalm 33:11 The plans of the LORD stand firm forever, and the purposes of His heart through all generations.

Welcome to Our House!

We Have a Special Gift for You

It is our privilege and pleasure to share in your love of Christian books. We are committed to bringing you authors and books that feed, challenge, and enrich your faith.

To show our appreciation, we invite you to sign up to receive a specially selected **Reader Appreciation Gift**, with our compliments. Just go to the Web address at the bottom of this page.

God bless you as you seek a deeper walk with Him!

WE HAVE A GIFT FOR YOU. VISIT:

whpub.me/nonfictionthx

WHITAKER HOUSE